Jan. 13, 1979

Bob, Liz, Tom & oy
Thank you for all
your concern, kindness
and generosity. You'll
always be in my
prayers. Keep me
in yours.
God Bless,
Father Clyde on
Philippines

PICTURE IDENTIFICATION - [All pictures are at the National Shrine of Our Lady of the Snows, Belleville, Ill.] - Inside Cover: left page, Outdoor Altar; right page, Annunciation Garden; upper left, wall behind Outdoor Altar; lower left, Christ the King Chapel.

THE SHRINE'S EVERYDAY PRAYER BOOK

THE MISSIONARY OBLATES OF MARY IMMACULATE

THE REVEREND OBLATE FATHERS
SHRINE OF OUR LADY OF THE SNOWS
BELLEVILLE, ILL. 62223

TABLE OF CONTENTS

7

THE WAY OF THE CROSS

THE SACRAMENT OF
RECONCILIATION

PRAYERS FOR SPECIAL INTENTIONS

PRAYERS OF RECONCILIATION
RECONCILIATION WITH GOD

RECONCILIATION WITH SELF

RECONCILIATION IN THE CHURCH

INTRODUCTION

There are two ways in which we may pray: the first is from the abundance of our heart and mind; the second is the use of external assistance through prayers that have been written by others.

The second way is by far the one used most frequently. Many of us need some assistance to carry on our conversation with Almighty God, His Blessed Mother and the Saints.

We at the Shrine of Our Lady of the Snows have seen this need and have produced this book of prayers to assist you in your devotions. I would especially like to thank Fr. John Maronic, OMI, and Fr. Mike Hanson, OMI, who have authored many of the prayers used in this book. I recommend this book to you to inspire you in faith, to strengthen your hope, and enkindle in your heart the fire of divine love.

Father Edwin J. Guild, OMI

MORNING PRAYER

O Lord, open my lips and my mouth will sing out your praise. Glory be to the Father, and to the Son, and to the Holy Spirit as it was in the beginning, is now, and ever shall be, world without end. Amen.

PSALM 5

Yahweh, let my words come to your ears, spare a thought for my sighs. Listen to my cry for help, my King and my God! I say this prayer to you, Yahweh, for at daybreak you listen for my voice; and at dawn I hold myself in readiness for you, I watch for you. You are not a God who is pleased with wickedness, you have no room for the wicked; boasters collapse under your scrutiny. You hate all evil men, liars you destroy; murderers and frauds Yahweh detests. But I, so great is your love, may come to your house, and before your holy Temple bow down in reverence to you. Yahweh, lead me in the path of your righteousness, for there are men lying in wait for me; make your way plain before me. Not a word from their lips can be trusted, deep within them lies ruin, their throats are yawning graves; they make their tongues so smooth! Pronounce them guilty, God, make their intrigues their own downfall! Hound them for their countless crimes, since they have rebelled against you. But joy for all who take shelter in you, endless shouts of joy! Since you protect them, they exult in you, those who love your name. It is you who bless the virtuous man, Yahweh; your favour is like a shield covering him.

(Any other psalm may be substituted)

PSALM-PRAYER

Lord Jesus, you bless the virtuous and humble man and hold contempt for the pride of hypocrites. Help me to be truthful and humble today and to follow your example of love for all.

MORNING CANTICLE

Blessed be the Lord, the God of Israel, for
    He has visited His people,
He has come to their rescue,
and He has raised up for us a power for
    salvation
in the House of His servant David,
even as He proclaimed,
by the mouth of His holy prophets from
    ancient times,
that He would save us from our enemies and
    from the hands of all who hate us.
Thus He shows mercy to our ancestors, thus
    He remembers His holy covenant,
the oath He swore to our father, Abraham,
that He would grant us, free from fear,
to be delivered from the hands of our ene-
    mies,
to serve Him in holiness and virtue in His
    presence, all our days.
And you, little child, you shall be called the
    Prophet of the Most High,
for you will go before the Lord to prepare
    the way for Him:
To give His people knowledge of salvation

through the forgiveness of their sins;
this by the tender mercy of our God
who from on high will bring the rising Sun
 to visit us,
to give light to those who live in darkness
 and the shadow of death,
and to guide our feet into the way of peace.

CONCLUDING PRAYERS

A special prayer for each day is now said.
It can be found in the pages that follow.
Morning prayer is then concluded with:

OUR FATHER   (page: 64)

The Lord bless us and keep us!
The Lord let His face shine upon us
and be gracious to us!
The Lord look upon us kindly
and give us peace! Amen.

Praise and thanksgiving be to you, Lord
Jesus Christ.

MORNING PRAYERS

SUNDAY: RECONCILIATION

This morning I pray in celebration of the fact that God continues to give His gifts of forgiveness and reconciliation. I pray that I may always be open to receiving these gifts and say: Lord, bring us together.

That the Holy Father's call to reconciliation may be heeded by all men and that everyone will seek the reconciliation which only God can give: Lord, bring us together.

That the whole Church may be open to renewal and reconciliation and may proclaim throughout the world the unity of all men in Christ: Lord, bring us together.

That each of us may work in unity with one another and with Christ to achieve lasting reconciliation in love: Lord, bring us together.

That I might come to know myself better and to appreciate what I am. That I might be reconciled within myself: Lord, bring us together.

That all people may learn to reconcile themselves with one another and that those
who have experienced war and conflict
may learn to reconcile themselves with
their memories: Lord, bring us together.
That the aged and afflicted and those close
to death may grow in their unity with
Christ: Lord, bring us together.

(Other prayers may be added)

Lord, help us to achieve true reconciliation
with God, with one another and with the
world around us. Help us to accept our unity
with Christ as He draws all things to Himself. And grant us the willingness to go out
of ourselves to achieve peace and harmony
with others. In Jesus' name, Amen.

MONDAY: THANKSGIVING

The greatest sign of our Christian love is our
gratitude to God and to others who have
shown their love to us. I pray this morning
in thanksgiving for all the good things I've
received: for the graces of God, the friendship of my brothers and sisters in Christ and

the blessings of the created world. Lord, I thank you.

For the beauty and goodness of the created universe: Lord, I thank you.

For history, the present day and the future: Lord, I thank you.

For the mysteries of your incarnation, your saving death, and your resurrection: Lord, I thank you.

For the genuine affection of others: Lord, I thank you.

For the appreciation of others for the things I've done for them: Lord, I thank you.

For the beauty of family life and especially for my own family: Lord, I thank you.

For touching me with morning skies, flowers, friendships and your own merciful love: Lord, I thank you.

(Other prayers may be added)

Lord, I am grateful for all the blessings you have given me. Help me to be appreciative always and to do my best to extend a helping hand to others – especially to those who find it difficult to say, "Thanks!" I pray in the name of Jesus. Amen.

TUESDAY: REPARATION

This morning, Lord, I pray for forgiveness and resolve to amend my life by repairing the damage caused by my sin. I pray that you will bless me with love, patience, forgiveness and a spirit of reparation and I say: Lord, show me the way.

That I may learn the uselessness of my hatreds, my anger and my selfish pride: Lord, show me the way.

That I may truly forgive all those who have injured me: Lord, show me the way.

That I may learn to accept graciously the apologies of those who have hurt me: Lord, show me the way.

That I may make up fully for the injury I've inflicted on others: Lord, show me the way.

That I may renounce sin and live up to the promises of amendment which I make to God: Lord, show me the way.

That I may be pardoned for all my evil thoughts, words and actions: Lord, show me the way.

That all those who are victims of oppression and injustice may pardon their oppressors and that those who oppress others may experience your grace and make amends: Lord, show me the way.

(Other prayers may be added)

Lord, grant me the grace to love all my brothers and sisters as you love me. Help me to make true reparation for my sins against them and against God. I ask this in your name. Amen.

WEDNESDAY: CHRISTIAN LIVING

Lord, I am a member of your Church and I call myself, "Christian." I pray this morning that I may be a worthy member of that Church and likewise may be worthy to bear the name of Christ. Lord, that I may live.

That I may receive an increase of faith and that my faith may be an example and an inspiration for many: Lord, that I may live.

That by living in the light of hope I may always trust in the goodness of God: Lord, that I may live.

That by my love I may warm those who are cold, comfort those who are afflicted and fill those who are empty: Lord, that I may live.

That I may be ever more generous in sharing myself and my possessions with others: Lord, that I may live.

That I may be courageous in my fidelity to Christ and to His Church: Lord, that I may live.

That as a Christian I may recognize and fulfill my role in the mission of the Church by bringing peace and justice to my home, to my vocation and to my neighborhood: Lord, that I may live.

(Other prayers may be added)

Lord, you said that your disciples would be recognized by their love. Teach me to love so that all may know that I am a Christian and that I may be truly your disciple. I pray in Jesus' name. Amen.

THURSDAY: SALVATION

This is the acceptable time! This is the day of salvation! Help me, Lord, to live a truly Christian life today in order that I may come closer to salvation. In your saving love, grant the requests I make today. Lord, grant salvation to all.

Lord, by my baptism I have died to sin and risen to a new life. Teach me to walk in the newness of life: Lord, grant salvation to all.

You went about doing good works for all men. Help me to do the same by participating in your work of salvation: Lord, grant salvation to all.

Help me, Lord, to work together with others to build up the "earthly city", that I may be in some way worthy of entering the "heavenly city": Lord, grant salvation to all.

You gave up your life for the salvation of the world. Help me to accept suffering and sacrifice that I may participate in that salvation: Lord, grant salvation to all.

Lord Jesus, be mindful of those who even now reject your salvation, pay no attention to it and live without hope. Grant them the added grace to come into your light: Lord, grant salvation to all.

Grant that those who have died, especially those who are my friends, may enter now into the full joy of your salvation: Lord, grant salvation to all.

(Other prayers may be added)

I look forward, Lord, to everlasting life with you. Help me today and everyday to live my earthly life more fully in order that I may have a greater share in the joy of heaven. I ask this through Christ, our Lord. Amen.

FRIDAY: THE WORLD

This morning I pray for the world in which I live, in thanksgiving for the gifts of creation and for the talents of mankind. I also pray for the preservation of its beauty and for the building up of a "new creation". Lord, make all things new again.

That those who are in a position of influence in our society may always put the dignity of man ahead of technological progress: Lord, make all things new again.

That our government and economic leaders may strive to preserve the beauty of nature and our national heritage: Lord, make all things new again.

That our world may experience the lasting peace which comes from love and may be freed from the devastation of war and natural disasters: Lord, make all things new again.

That the earth may remain fertile to provide food for all men: Lord, make all things new again.

That we may work diligently to transform the created world in order that it might serve us better: Lord, make all things new again.

That those who live in slums, in poverty, in destitution may be elevated to a better way of life: Lord, make all things new again.

That we may always trust in Divine Providence and recognize that many of the solutions to problems which trouble us are found not here but in heaven: Lord, make all things new again.

(Other prayers may be added)

Lord, grant that we may all benefit from the fruits of science, technology and ecology. But, at the same time, help us to avoid making these things our gods. Thank you for the whole of the created universe and for the wisdom of men who transform it for our benefit. Grant that by living in the fullness of earthly life we may all come to live in the fuller life of heaven. In Jesus' name, Amen.

SATURDAY: MARY

With the love of a mother, Mary looks upon our troubled world and upon our Chrurch. We join her in prayer, saying: Mary, Mother of the Church, intercede for us.

That the Church may continue the work of reconciliation begun by Christ: Mary, Mother of the Church, intercede for us.

That each of us may share Mary's faith in her son, Jesus, and may follow God's will with joy: Mary, Mother of the Church, intercede for us.

That as Mary's body became the dwelling place of God, we may all become temples of the Holy Spirit: Mary, Mother of the Church, intercede for us.

For all mothers, living and dead, that God may reward them for the sacrifices they have made for their children: Mary, Mother of the Church, intercede for us.

For those who will be mothers, that they may share Mary's love for life and life of love: Mary, Mother of the Church, intercede for us.

For all those who are unaware of Mary's maternal love for them, that they may recognize her as their own mother: Mary, Mother of the Church, intercede for us.

For all the People of God that they may come to the life of glory promised to mankind in the assumption of Mary: Mary, Mother of the Church, intercede for us.

(Other prayers may be added)

Mary, mother of God and our own mother, we pray today that you will be aware of all our needs and will continue to intercede on our behalf as we beg for the mercy and blessings of your son, Jesus Christ, our Lord. Amen.

THE ANGELUS

V. The Angel of the Lord declared unto Mary.

R. And she conceived of the Holy Spirit. Hail Mary...

V. Behold the handmaid of the Lord.

R. Be it done unto me according to Your Word.   Hail Mary...

V. And the Word was made flesh.

R. And dwelled among us.   Hail Mary...

V. Pray for us, O holy Mother of God.

R. That we may be made worthy of the promises of Christ.

LET US PRAY:

Pour forth, we beseech you, O Lord, your grace into our hearts, that we, to whom the

Incarnation of Christ your Son was made known by the message of an angel, may, by His Passion and Cross, be brought to the glory of His Resurrection. Through the same Christ our Lord.   Amen.

V.   Glory be to the Father, and to the Son, and to the Holy Spirit.

R.   As it was in the beginning, is now, and ever shall be, world without end. Amen.

REGINA CAELI

O Queen of Heaven, rejoice; alleluia,
The Son Whom it was your privilege to
  bear;   alleluia,
Has risen as He said;   alleluia:
Pray to God for us;   alleluia.
V.   Rejoice and be glad, O Virgin Mary;
  alleluia.
R.   For the Lord has truly risen;   alleluia.

LET US PRAY:

O God, You were pleased to give joy to the
world through the resurrection of Your Son,
our Lord Jesus Christ; grant, we beseech

You, that through His Mother, the Virgin Mary, we may obtain the joys of everlasting life. Through the same Christ our Lord. Amen.

V. Glory be to the Father, and to the Son, and to the Holy Spirit.
R. As it was in the beginning, is now, and ever shall be, world without end. Amen.

To be said in place of the Angelus during the Easter Season...

EVENING PRAYER

O God, come to my aid. Lord, hasten to help me.
Glory be to the Father, and to the Son, and to the Holy Spirit as it was in the beginning, is now, and ever shall be. Amen.

(Examination of conscience)

PSALM 4

God, guardian of my rights, you answer when I call, when I am in trouble, you come to my relief; now be good to me and hear my prayer. You men, why shut your hearts so long, loving delusions, chasing after lies. Know this, Yahweh works wonders for those he loves, Yahweh hears me when I call to him. Tremble: give up sinning, spend your night in quiet meditation. Offer sacrifice in a right spirit, and trust Yahweh. "Who will give us sight of happiness?" many say. Show us the light of your face, turned towards us! Yahweh, you have given more joy to my heart than others ever knew, for all their corn and wine. In peace I lie down, and fall asleep at once, since you alone, Yahweh, make me rest secure.

(Any other psalm may be substituted)

PSALM-PRAYER

Lord Jesus, you instructed us to be like the lilies of the field and the birds of the air, trusting in the Father's goodness and providence. I turn to you this evening in complete trust and confidence. I offer you all the good things I did today and ask you to protect me this night, that I might rise tomorrow to do your will. Amen.

EVENING CANTICLE

My soul proclaims the greatness of the Lord
and my spirit exults in God my savior;
because He has looked upon His lowly handmaid.
Yes, from this day forward all generations
will call me blessed,
for the Almighty has done great things for
me.
Holy is His name,
and His mercy reaches from age to age for
those who fear Him.
He has shown the power of His arm, He
has routed the proud of heart.
He has pulled down princes from their
thrones and exalted the lowly.
The hungry He has filled with good things,
the rich sent empty away.
He has come to the help of Israel, His servant,
mindful of His mercy
–according to the promise He made to our
ancestors–
of His mercy to Abraham and to His descen-
dants forever.

THE CONFITEOR

I confess to almighty God,
and to you, my brothers and sisters,
that I have sinned through my own fault,
in my thoughts and in my words,
in what I have done,
and in what I have failed to do;
and I ask blessed Mary, ever virgin,
all the angels and saints,
and you, my brothers and sisters,
to pray for me to the Lord our God.

May almighty God have mercy on us,
forgive us our sins,
and bring us to everlasting life.

Amen.

PRAYER TO CHRIST THE KING

O Christ Jesus, I acknowledge You as Universal King. All that has been made, was created for You. Exercise over me all the rights that You have.

I renew my baptismal promises, renouncing Satan, his pomps and his works, and I promise to live as a good Christian. Especially do I pledge myself by all the means in my power to bring about the triumph of the rights of God and of Your Church.

Divine Heart of Jesus, I offer You my poor actions to obtain that all hearts may recognize Your consecrated Kingship and that thus the Kingdom of Your peace may be established in the whole world. Amen.

PSALM 23

THE GOOD SHEPHERD

Yahweh is my shepherd,
  I lack nothing.

In meadows of green grass he lets me lie.

To the waters of repose he leads me;
  there he revives my soul.

He guides me by paths of virtue
  for the sake of his name.

Though I pass through a gloomy valley,
  I fear no harm;
beside me your rod and your staff
  are there, to hearten me.

You prepare a table before me
    under the eyes of my enemies;
you anoint my head with oil,
    my cup brims over.

Ah, how goodness and kindness pursue me,
    every day of my life;
my home, the house of Yahweh,
    as long as I live!

THE CANTICLE OF MARY

My soul proclaims the greatness of the
  Lord
    and my spirit exults in God my savior;
    because he has looked upon his lowly
      handmaid.
Yes, from this day forward all generations
    will call me blessed,
    for the Almighty has done great things
      for me.
Holy is his name,
    and his mercy reaches from age to age
      for those who fear him.

He has shown the power of his arm,
   he has routed the proud of heart.
He has pulled down princes from their
      thrones and exalted the lowly.
The hungry he has filled with good things,
      the rich sent empty away.
He has come to the help of Israel his
      servant, mindful of his mercy
—according to the promise he made to
      our ancestors—
of his mercy to Abraham and to his
      descendants for ever.

Luke 1:11-55

THE CANTICLE OF SIMEON

Now, Master, you can let your servant
    go in peace, just as you promised;
because my eyes have seen the salvation
which you have prepared for all the
    nations to see,
a light to enlighten the pagans
and the glory of your people Israel.

Luke 2:29-32

WE FLY TO YOUR PATRONAGE

We fly to your patronage, O Holy Mother of God; despise not our petitions in our necessities; but ever deliver us from all dangers, O glorious and blessed Virgin.

EVENING PRAYERS

SUNDAY: CONVERSION OF HEART

This evening, Lord, I pray for a sinful world, a world that needs a true conversion of heart, a world composed of men and women who are in need of reconciliation with God and with one another. Lord, grant us a change of heart.

That people who are filled with selfish pride may discover in humility who and what they truly are: Lord, grant us a change of heart.

That people who are greedy for material possessions may realize the emptiness of slavery to things: Lord, grant us a change of heart.

That people who are filled with anger may find in tolerance the ability to accept their own frailties and those of others: Lord, grant us a change of heart.

That people who suffer from envy and jealousy may turn to joy in the good fortune of others: Lord, grant us a change of heart.

That people who could care less about God may turn to Him in prayer: Lord, grant us a change of heart.

(Other prayers may be added)

Lord, all too often, I am that selfish, greedy, angry, envious and indifferent person for whom I have just prayed. Grant me the grace of conversion that I may turn to you and renew my pledge of love. I ask this in your name, Lord Jesus. Amen.

MONDAY: LIBERATION

I pray this evening, Lord, for the great gift of liberation. I seek freedom from the things that oppress me and keep me away from you. I seek freedom to renew my Christian life in reconciling myself to you and to others. Lord, grant us freedom.

That the Church may be liberated from the scandal of disunity: Lord, grant us freedom.

That the people who have not yet come to the knowledge of Christ may be freed from the darkness of ignorance and superstition: Lord, grant us freedom.

That the oppressed minorities in our society may be liberated from injustice, especially from discrimination based on race, religion, sex and the like: Lord, grant us freedom.

That living conditions in prisons may be improved and that prisoners may find God in their lives: Lord, grant us freedom.

That the sick and the suffering and especially those close to death may unite themselves with the suffering Christ and rise to new life in Him: Lord, grant us freedom.

That all of us may accept the liberation from sin and death won for us on the cross: Lord, grant us freedom.

(Other prayers may be added)

Lord, you brought us freedom in the Paschal Mystery of your suffering, death and resurrection. Help us to accept that freedom and to extend it through the Church to all men. I ask this in Jesus' name. Amen.

TUESDAY: JUSTICE

I pray for justice this evening, Lord. I pray in sorrow for the times I have unjustly harmed another. I pray in concern for all who are oppressed. Lord, help me help another.

That I may constantly be aware of the presence of Christ in my brothers and sisters: Lord, help me help another.

That I may not shut my eyes to the misery of those around me, but may work to comfort them: Lord, help me help another.

That I may strive to assist the needy not only with money but also with joy, love, concern, hope and peace: Lord, help me help another.

That I may banish all prejudice, injustice, envy and hatred from my heart: Lord, help me help another.

That I may learn to share the blessings God has given me with others: Lord, help me help another.

That I may never fear to "get involved": Lord, help me help another.

(Other prayers may be added)

Jesus, you came into the world to bring peace and justice to all men. You have called me, as a Christian, to share in that missionary work. Help me to help those around me. I ask this, Lord, in your name. Amen.

WEDNESDAY: LOVE

Lord, this evening, I pray for the kind of outgoing love that can transform the world, the kind of love that seeks to reconcile all things in Christ. I pray for a love that asks little but seeks to do much. Lord, teach me to love.

That I may learn to love others as you love them: Lord, teach me to love.

That I may learn from my experience of human love to know the love of God and to love Him above all: Lord, teach me to love.

That I may better understand and practice the command of Christ to love my enemies: Lord, teach me to love.

That I may learn to realize how much I need others: Lord, teach me to love.

That I may learn to realize how much others need me: Lord, teach me to love.

That my love for others may be sincere, affectionate, strong and pure: Lord, teach me to love.

That my love may bring me to everlasting joyful life with you: Lord, teach me to love.

(Other prayers may be added)

Lord, you taught us to love God above all things and our neighbors as ourselves. Let me love wisely and well, so that the world may know that I am your disciple. Let me lead others to you in love. In Jesus' name, Amen.

THURSDAY: ECUMENISM

Jesus prayed, "That they all be one." This evening I join my prayer to His, asking the Holy Spirit of unity and love to unite all men to Christ. I pray for the peace, well-being and unity of the Church. Holy Spirit, unite us.

That all the leaders of the Church may receive God's favor in their apostolic efforts towards unity: Holy Spirit, unite us.

That we may find unity in our own families and extend that familial unity to the Church: Holy Spirit, unite us.

That all Christians may again be united in the one Body of Christ and proclaim His message of one baptism, one faith and one God who is Father: Holy Spirit, unite us.

That non-Christians and non-believers may receive the gospel message and accept it with love: Holy Spirit, unite us.

That, united in Christ, all of us may strive to respond as He did to the poor, the underprivileged and the oppressed: Holy Spirit, unite us.

That wars, hatred and enmity may be banished by the Christian spirit of unity, love and peace: Holy Spirit, unite us.

(Other prayers may be added)

Jesus, you are the one shepherd and we, your flock, are scattered. Gather us together again in the one fold and help us to follow in your way. Amen.

FRIDAY: RENEWAL

Lord, this evening I recognize that my days are constantly filled with new beginnings. I pray for the grace to grasp the opportunities for renewal. I pray for renewal for myself and for those who are as weak as I am. Lord, renew us in love.

That Christian people may treasure faith in God above all past tradition and future plans and that Church renewal may inspire individual renewal: Lord, renew us in love.

That world governments may begin to build again where war and enmity have wreaked devastation; that unity, peace and justice may be renewed: Lord, renew us in love.

That though many of us fall in sin we may be renewed in life through the sacraments that reconcile us to God: Lord, renew us in love.

That I may correct my own failings and renew my faithfulness, my sincerity and my love: Lord, renew us in love.

That God will continue to renew His covenant of love with His People and that I may respond to that covenant love with my own love: Lord, renew us in love.

(Other prayers may be added)

Lord, grant me the grace of renewing my commitment to you. Let me renew my life now in order that I may come to a future new life with you. I ask this in your name. Amen.

SATURDAY: FAMILY

It is said, Lord, that a society is only as strong as its families. This may give us pause to wonder about the society we find ourselves in today. And so I pray for my own family and for all the families in the world. Lord, bless our homes.

That the Church may continue to support the family unit and may find in the family a model for its own unity: Lord, bless our homes.

That Christian families may be especially close and loving so as to set an example for all families: Lord, bless our homes.

That families which are separated or experiencing great problems may find unity in the love of parents and children: Lord, bless our homes.

That all families may be blessed with stability, love, warmth and unity: Lord, bless our homes.

That all nations of the world may become a family of peoples and find support from the homes that comprise them: Lord, bless our homes.

(Other prayers may be added)

Lord, you grew up in a holy family and called all of us your brothers and sisters. Under the protection of our mother, Mary, bring us all safely to our heavenly home. We ask this in the name of Jesus Christ, our Lord. Amen.

AN ACT OF FAITH

O My God! I firmly believe that You are one God in three Divine Persons, Father, Son, and Holy Spirit. I believe that Your Divine Son became man, and died for our sins, and that He will come to judge the living and the dead. I believe these and all the truths which the Holy Catholic Church teaches, because You have revealed them, Who can neither deceive nor be deceived.

AN ACT OF HOPE

O my God! Relying upon Your infinite goodness and promises, I hope to obtain pardon for my sins, the help of Your grace, and life everlasting, through the merits of Jesus Christ, my Lord and Redeemer.

AN ACT OF LOVE

O My God! I love you above all things with my whole heart and soul, because you are all-good and worthy of all love. I love my neighbor as myself for the love of you. I forgive all who have injured me, and ask pardon of all whom I have injured.

THE ROSARY

PRAYING THE ROSARY

The complete rosary is prayed by reciting the introductory prayers and fifteen decades of the beads. While reciting the prayers, one reflects on the history of salvation from the announcement of Christ's birth to the coronation of Mary.

One begins praying the rosary by holding the crucifix and reciting the "Apostle's Creed." The "Lord's Prayer" is then recited on the first bead. Some make it a practice to reflect on the Trinity at this point. The "Hail Mary" is recited on each of the three smaller beads. Some reflect at this time on the Father, Son and Holy Spirit; others, on the virtues of faith, hope and charity. The "Doxology" is sometimes added after the third "Hail Mary."

On the next bead, the first decade begins with the recitation of the "Lord's Prayer." Each decade of "Hail Mary's" is preceded by the "Lord's Prayer," and it is customary to conclude each decade with a recitation of the "Doxology," although no beads are supplied for this prayer. Some also add, after the "Doxology," the short prayer: "O Jesus, forgive us our sins, save us from the fires of hell and lead all souls to heaven, especially those who are most in need of your mercy."

It is customary to end the recitation of the rosary by praying the "Hail, Holy Queen." This prayer is used at the conclusion of the recitation even when only five decades are prayed. The praying of five decades is a common practice.

"Mystery" is the name given to an event of salvation history. There are fifteen decades, each dedicated to a specific mystery. These are divided into groups of five, under the titles of "Joyful", "Sorrowful" and "Glorious."

Some people make it a practice in praying the daily rosary to reflect on the Joyful Mysteries on Monday and Thursday, the Sorrowful Mysteries on Tuesday and Friday, and the Glorious Mysteries on Wednesday, Saturday, and Sunday. It is also traditional to use the Joyful Mysteries on the Sundays of Advent and Christmastide, and the Sorrowful Mysteries on the Sundays of Lent. The rosary is both a recitative and meditative praying experience. The recited prayers are these:

APOSTLE'S CREED

I believe in God, the Father Almighty,
    Creator of heaven and earth;
And in Jesus Christ, His only Son, our Lord;
Who was conceived by the Holy Spirit,
Born of the Virgin Mary,
Suffered under Pontius Pilate,
Was crucified, died, and was buried.
He descended into hell;
The third day He rose again from the dead.
He ascended into heaven,
    sitteth at the right hand of God,
    the Father Almighty.
From thence He shall come to judge
    the living and the dead.
I believe in the Holy Spirit,
    the holy catholic Church,
    the communion of saints,
    the forgiveness of sins,
    the resurrection of the body,
    and life everlasting. Amen.

OUR FATHER

Our Father, who art in heaven,
   hallowed be thy name;
Thy kingdom come;
Thy will be done, on earth
   as it is in heaven.
Give us this day our daily bread;
And forgive us our trespasses
   as we forgive those
   who trespass against us;
And lead us not into temptation,
But deliver us from evil. Amen.

HAIL MARY

Hail Mary, full of grace,
   the Lord is with thee;
Blessed art thou among women;
And blessed is the fruit
   of thy womb, Jesus.
Holy Mary, Mother of God,
   pray for us sinners,
   now and at the hour
   of our death. Amen.

DOXOLOGY

Glory be to the Father,
   and to the Son,
   and to the Holy Spirit;
As it was in the beginning,
   is now, and ever shall be,
   world without end. Amen.

HAIL, HOLY QUEEN

Hail, Holy Queen, Mother of Mercy.
   our life, our sweetness and our hope!
To you do we cry,
   poor banished children of Eve!
To you do we send up our sighs;
   mourning and weeping
   in this vale of tears!
Turn then, most gracious advocate,
   your eyes of mercy toward us;
   and after this, our exile,
   show to us the blessed fruit
   of your womb, Jesus!
O clement, O loving, O sweet Virgin
   Mary!

THE ROSARY OF OUR LADY

The custom of using beads while praying goes back for centuries and is still used by many of the oriental religions.

The Rosary evolved in the history of prayer in the Church as the layman's breviary. The monks and priests in the monasteries recited so many psalms each day, while the workers in the field or the domestics doing their chores united with them by telling their beads in numbers which matched the psalms. When Saint Dominic came along to preach a "Crusade of Prayer" for an agonizing and afflicted Church, the form of the Rosary as we know it came into being. It became very popular and widespread. It has been approved and acclaimed by the Church as a rich and meaningful form of prayer.

The idea of the Rosary being a kind of Office for the laity is still a valid one. With the Rosary we are praying with the Christ-Priest as we meditate on the scenes and mysteries of His life. We are also praying with the Church for all her needs and the needs of her children. We must feel with and for the

Church as she, the Body of Christ, goes through His mysteries of joys, sorrows and triumphs with the passing of ages.

Here in this booklet we set up a series of thought patterns to help you pray the Rosary better. Each mystery is developed in such a way as to nourish and sustain meditation on your own. As the beads roll through the fingers, the thoughts roll through the mind and heart. This gives direction to our thoughts and purpose to our prayer.

It is our hope that gradually you may develop your own series of thoughts in connection with the Rosary. May you thus uncover its true riches as a spring watering your own prayer life and a school of holiness.

THE JOYFUL MYSTERIES

1. THE ANNUNCIATION

In the sixth month the angel Gabriel was sent by God to a town in Galilee called Nazareth, to a virgin betrothed to a man named Joseph, of the House of David; and the virgin's name was Mary. He went in and said to her, 'Rejoice, so highly favoured! The Lord is with you.' She was deeply disturbed by these words and asked herself what this greeting could mean, but the angel said to her, 'Mary, do not be afraid; you have won God's favor. Listen! You are to conceive and bear a son, and you must name him Jesus. He will be great and will be called Son of the Most High. The Lord God will give him the throne of his ancestor David; he will rule over the House of Jacob for ever and his reign will have no end.' Mary said to the angel, 'But how can this come about, since I am a virgin?' 'The Holy Spirit will come upon you' the angel answered 'and the power of the Most High will cover you with its shadow. And so the child will be holy and will be called Son of God. Know this too; your kinswoman Elizabeth has, in her old age, herself conceived a son, and she whom people called barren is now in her sixth month, for nothing is impossible to God.' 'I am the handmaid of the Lord,' said Mary 'let what you have said be done to me.'

Luke 1:26-38

2. THE VISITATION

Mary set out at that time and went as quickly as she could to a town in the hill country of Judah. She went into Zechariah's house and greeted Elizabeth. Now as soon as Elizabeth heard Mary's greeting, the child leapt in her womb and Elizabeth was filled with the Holy Spirit. She gave a loud cry and said, 'Of all women you are the most blessed, and blessed is the fruit of your womb. Why should I be honoured with a visit from the mother of my Lord? For the moment your greeting reached my ears, the child in my womb leapt for joy. Yes, blessed is she who believed that the promise made her by the Lord would be fulfilled.'

Luke 1:39-45

3. THE BIRTH OF JESUS

So Joseph set out from the town of Nazareth in Galilee and travelled up to Judaea, to the town of David called Bethlehem, since he was of David's House and line, in order to be registered together with Mary, his betrothed, who was with child. While they were there the time came for her to have her child, and she gave birth to a son, her first-born. She wrapped him in swaddling clothes, and laid him in a manger because there was no room for them at the inn. In the countryside close by there were shepherds who lived in the fields and took it in turns to watch their flocks during the night. The angel of the Lord appeared to them and the glory of the Lord shone round them. They were terrified, but the angel said, 'Do not be afraid. Listen, I bring you news of great joy, a joy to be shared by the whole people. Today in the town of David a savior has been born to you; he is Christ the Lord. And here is a sign for you; you will find a baby wrapped in swaddling clothes and lying in a manger.'

Luke 2:4-13

4. THE PRESENTATION
OF JESUS IN THE TEMPLE

And when the day came for them to be purified as laid down by the Law of Moses, they took him up to Jerusalem to present him to the Lord.

As the child's father and mother stood there wondering at the things that were being said about him, Simeon blessed them and said to Mary his mother, 'You see this child: he is destined for the fall and for the rising of many in Israel, destined to be a sign that is rejected —and a sword will pierce your own soul too— so that the secret thoughts of many may be laid bare'.

Luke 2:22, 33-35

THE JOYFUL MYSTERIES

5. FINDING OF JESUS IN THE TEMPLE

Every year his parents used to go to Jerusalem for the feast of the Passover. When he was twelve years old, they went up for the feast as usual. When they were on their way home after the feast, the boy Jesus stayed behind in Jerusalem without his parents knowing it. They assumed he was with the caravan, and it was only after a day's journey that they went to look for him among their relations and acquaintances. When they failed to find him they went back to Jerusalem looking for him everywhere.

Three days later, they found him in the Temple, sitting among the doctors, listening to them, and asking them questions; and all those who heard him were astounded at his intelligence and his replies. They were overcome when they saw him, and his mother said to him, 'My child, why have you done this to us? See how worried your father and I have been, looking for you.' 'Why were you looking for me?' he replied 'Did you not know that I must be busy with my Father's affairs?' But they did not understand what he meant.

Luke 2:41-50

THE SORROWFUL MYSTERIES

1. THE AGONY IN THE GARDEN

He then left to make his way as usual to the Mount of Olives, with the disciples following. When they reached the place he said to them, 'Pray not to be put to the test'.

Then he withdrew from them, about a stone's throw away, and knelt down and prayed. 'Father,' he said 'if you are willing, take this cup away from me... Nevertheless, let your will be done, not mine.' Then an angel appeared to him, coming from heaven to give him strength. In his anguish he prayed even more earnestly, and his sweat fell to the ground like great drops of blood.

Luke 22:39-46

THE SORROWFUL MYSTERIES

2. THE SCOURGING OF JESUS

At festival time Pilate used to release a prisoner for them, anyone they asked for. Now a man called Barabbas was then in prison with the rioters who had committed murder during the uprising. When the crowd went up and began to ask Pilate the customary favour, Pilate answered them, 'Do you want me to release for you the king of the Jews?' For he realized it was out of jealousy that the chief priests had handed Jesus over. The chief priests, however, had incited the crowd to demand that he should release Barabbas for them instead. Then Pilate spoke again. 'But in that case,' he said to them 'what am I to do with the man you call king of the Jews?' They shouted back, 'Crucify him!' 'Why?' Pilate asked them 'What harm has he done?' But they shouted all the louder, 'Crucify him!' So Pilate, anxious to placate the crowd, released Barabbas for them and, having ordered Jesus to be scourged, handed him over to be crucified.

Mark 15:1-16

THE SORROWFUL MYSTERIES

3. THE CROWNING
WITH THORNS

The soldiers led him away to the inner part of the palace, that is, the Praetorium, and called the whole cohort together. They dressed him up in purple, twisted some thorns into a crown and put it on him. And they began saluting him, 'Hail, king of the Jews!' They struck his head with a reed and spat on him; and they went down on their knees to do him homage. And when they had finished making fun of him, they took off the purple and dressed him in his own clothes.

Mark 15:16-20

THE SORROWFUL MYSTERIES

4. THE CARRYING
OF THE CROSS

As they were leading him away they seized on a man, Simon from Cyrene, who was coming in from the country, and made him shoulder the cross and carry it behind Jesus. Large numbers of people followed him, and of women too, who mourned and lamented for him. But Jesus turned to them and said, 'Daughters of Jerusalem, do not weep for me; weep rather for yourselves and for your children.

For the days will surely come when people will say, 'Happy are those who are barren, the wombs that have never borne, the breasts that have never suckled!' Then they will begin to say to the mountains, 'Fall on us!'; to the hills, 'Cover us!' For if men use the green wood like this, what will happen when it is dry?' Now with him they were also leading out two other criminals to be executed.

Luke 22:20-32

THE SORROWFUL MYSTERIES

5. THE CRUCIFIXION

When they reached the place called The Skull, they crucified him there and the two criminals also, one on the right, the other on the left. Jesus said, 'Father, forgive them; they do not know what they are doing'. Then they cast lots to share out his clothing.

The people stayed there watching him. As for the leaders, they jeered at him. 'He saved others,' they said 'let him save himself if he is the Christ of God, the Chosen One.' The soldiers mocked him too, and when they approached to offer him vinegar they said, 'If you are the King of the Jews, save yourself'. Above him there was an inscription: 'This is the king of the Jews'.

One of the criminals hanging there abused him. 'Are you not the Christ?' he said. 'Save yourself and us as well.' But the other spoke up and rebuked him, 'Have you no fear of God at all?' he said. 'You got the same sentence as he did, but in our case we deserved it: we are paying for what we did. But this man has done nothing wrong!' 'Jesus,' he said 'remember me when you come into your kingdom.' 'Indeed, I promise you,' he replied 'today you will be with me in paradise.'

It was now about the sixth hour and, with the sun eclipsed, a darkness came over the whole land until the ninth hour. The veil of the Temple was torn right down the middle; and when Jesus had cried out in a loud voice, he said, 'Father, into your hands I commit my spirit'. With these words he breathed his last.

Luke 23:33-46

THE GLORIOUS MYSTERIES

1. THE RESURRECTION

After the sabbath, and towards dawn on the first day of the week, Mary of Magdala and the other Mary went to visit the sepulchre. And all at once there was a violent earthquake, for the angel of the Lord, descending from heaven, came and rolled away the stone and sat on it. His face was like lightning, his robe white as snow. The guards were so shaken, so frightened of him, that they were like dead men. But the angel spoke; and he said to the women, 'There is no need for you to be afraid. I know you are looking for Jesus, who was crucified. He is not here, for he has risen, as he said he would. Come and see the place where he lay, then go quickly and tell his disciples, 'he has risen from the dead and now he is going before you to Galilee; it is there you will see him'. Now I have told you.' Filled with awe and great joy the women came quickly away from the tomb and ran to tell the disciples.

Matthew 28:1-8

THE GLORIOUS MYSTERIES

2. THE ASCENSION

Now having met together, they asked him, 'Lord, has the time come? Are you going to restore the kingdom to Israel?' He replied, 'It is not for you to know times or dates that the Father has decided by his own authority, but you will receive power when the Holy Spirit comes on you, and then you will be my witnesses not only in Jerusalem but throughout Judaea and Samaria, and indeed to the ends of the earth'. As he said this he was lifted up while they looked on, and a cloud took him from their sight. They were still staring into the sky when suddenly two men in white were standing near them and they said, 'Why are you men from Galilee standing here looking into the sky? Jesus who has been taken up from you into heaven, this same Jesus will come back in the same way as you have seen him go there.'

Acts 1:6-11

THE GLORIOUS MYSTERIES

3. THE DESCENT OF THE HOLY SPIRIT ON THE APOSTLES

When Pentecost day came round, they had all met in one room, when suddenly they heard what sounded like a powerful wind from heaven, the noise of which filled the entire house in which they were sitting; and something appeared to them that seemed like tongues of fire; these separated and came to rest on the head of each of them. They were all filled with the Holy Spirit, and began to speak foreign languages as the Spirit gave them the gift of speech.

Acts 2:1-4

THE GLORIOUS MYSTERIES

4. THE ASSUMPTION OF MARY INTO HEAVEN

The Assumption was a real event about which we should have no doubt; rather we should have for it in our faithful hearts certainty, joy, hope, seeking to understand the symbolic value which this miraculous fact holds in the economy of salvation and in Christian behavior.

The Assumption is the triumph not only of the most pure soul of her who was Blessed among women, but likewise of her innocent, virginal and immaculate body. Just as the body of Jesus, her Son, was raised from the dead and thus invested with the divinity to which it was united in order to enjoy a higher form of life, so the body of Mary most pure, which by the power of the Holy Spirit, had generated the humanity of Christ, attains that fullness of perfection which is reserved to bodies after the blessed resurrection. *(Cf. 1 Cor. 15:42ff)*

It is a programmatic lesson for us who, as children of our age, tend to materialize the human spirit and to subject it to the dominion of pleasure and the reign of the senses, by making of the flesh a temptation and a dark and illusory principle of corruption. On the other hand, Our Lady assumed into heaven gives us the vision of the spiritualization of the flesh by making it resplendent in purity and beauty. It is, as it were, an invitation to us to give back again to the corporeal part of our being its dignity and its title, that is, true purity, in order to recover the superhuman immortality of the resurrection and of eternal life.

Worldly opinion might regard all of this as unreal, like the voice of a dream, or something out of fashion, so much does the decadence of public morality preach and profess the contrary. Let us therefore, if we are possessed of the Christian sense, seek to restore to the body its true nobility which the spirit quickens and reinvigorates and, if necessary, chastens in order to insure reaching the goal of the eternal and happy resurrection.

May Our Lady assumed into heaven help us to relish physical purity and spiritual beauty.

...Pope Paul VI

THE GLORIOUS MYSTERIES

5. MARY IS CROWNED QUEEN OF HEAVEN AND EARTH

In the bodily and spiritual glory which she possesses in heaven, the Mother of Jesus continues in this present world as the image and first flowering of the Church as she is to be perfected in the world to come. Likewise, Mary shines forth on earth, until the day of the Lord shall come *(cf. 2 Pet. 3:10)*, as a sign of sure hope and solace for the pilgrim People of God.

Let the entire body of the faithful pour forth persevering prayer to the Mother of God and Mother of men. Let them implore that she who aided the beginnings of the

Church by her prayers may now, exalted as she is in heaven above all the saints and angels, intercede with her Son in the fellowship of all the saints. May she do so until all the people of the human family, whether they are honored with the name of Christian or whether they still do not know their Savior, are happily gathered together in peace and harmony into the one People of God, for the glory of the Most Holy and Undivided Trinity.

.... *Pope Paul VI*

NOVENA PRAYERS
TO OUR LADY OF THE SNOWS

Remember, O most gracious Virgin Mary, that never was it known that anyone who fled to thy protection, implored thy help or sought thy intercession, was left unaided. Inspired with this confidence, I fly unto thee, O Virgin of virgins, my Mother; to thee do I come, before thee I stand, sinful and sorrowful; O Mother of the Word Incarnate, despise not my petitions, but in thy mercy hear and answer me. Amen.

Our Father.
Hail Mary.
Our Lady of the Snows, pray for us.
St. Joseph, pray for us.
St. Therese, Patroness of the Missions, pray for us.
Glory be to the Father.

THE WAY OF THE CROSS

GOD'S WAY OF LOVE

PRELUDE

Here we are, Lord Jesus, walking the road to Calvary with you again. Help us to think out loud about our Passion and Resurrection, about our Church, the People of God, and about our beautiful world that is so often tainted by the greed of men.

Let your Spirit of wisdom and love penetrate our inner selves and take over our thoughts and affections. Help us realize that the passion is only one segment in the total picture of the mysteries of joys, sorrows and triumphs in the life of every person, and in the life of the Church and the world.

Our own trials become so deeply personal at times that we forget how they relate to the rest of our lives. Joy, sorrow, failure and triumph must be seen as parts of the whole pattern if they are to make any sense at all. We do not suffer only to suffer, but to prepare the way for the glories and delights of the kingdom of heaven, which in a real sense has already begun. Yes, here on earth we are already living the Paschal Mystery! You once said, "I have a baptism which I must encounter and I want so much to have it over with." That baptism is your total immersion into the heart of every man, a total identification with each person. It is in your passion and death that you reach the inner depths of each heart, and by your resurrection that you lift us out of ourselves. Now every person can immerse himself in you and identify with you entirely.

You became one of us so that we might become one with you. In so doing, we most surely become ourselves. That is the meaning of our baptism, isn't it? Paul said it for us, "We are baptized into your death, so that we might become alive in you." And then all the joys, risks and works of our personal lives become yours, you living in us and among us, and we living in you.

We are born again, not just by water, but by water and blood and the Spirit. We are washed clean by water, fed and consecrated by your flesh and blood, and enlivened by your Spirit.

All creation is thus redeemed and restored. When you were lifted up, you took it all to yourself, and in your own person are giving it back to our Father in heaven. This is the new creation! This is total reality!

May these sentiments be in our minds and hearts, and on our lips, as we experience this Passover from sin and death into the new life and resurrection with you.

THE FIRST STATION

Jesus is condemned to death.

FIRST STATION:

DEFENSELESS

Lord Jesus, you stand in judgment before the whole world. You undergo all the rank injustice of a law which is handled by vicious men.

You are innocence in person, yet stand condemned! "For which of my good deeds are you trying to kill me?" you ask. And we have no answer.

Yes, we have no answer except that somehow you had to take the place of each one of those millions of people who would be enslaved by others, in slums and ghettoes, in prison camps and slave labor gangs, in poverty and misery and violence, all the walls of cruelty which men build in their hearts against their fellowmen.

You have been through inner city and skid row to identify with the public sinners and the outcasts. Now you go into death-row itself to identify with one of the most abandoned of all, the convicted criminal.

Our age is called an age of progress and civilization, yet it is barbaric with poverty, hunger and slavery, so unnecessary because of our technology, yet perpetuated by fear and greed and thoughtlessness.

Because of what you went through here for us, we are becoming more aware of each other's needs, more human. The barriers of race and color and sophistication are breaking down. The Christian message is slowly getting through.

At times we do forget and become like Pilate sitting in judgment on others, but we regret it, especially when we hear your words of warning: "What you have done to the least of these, you have done to me!"

We begin to understand, dear Lord, that you have identified with every person, that whoever does the least service to one of your 'Little Ones' does it to you personally, that he who does the will of the Father in heaven is indeed your brother and sister, your father and mother.

Teach us to love them all as People of God, and to love singly and fully each one you bring across our pathway in life.

How to Say the Rosary

THE ROSARY is a form of vocal and mental prayer on the Mysteries of our Redemption, divided into fifteen decades.

The recitation of each decade is accompanied by meditation on one of the fifteen events or "mysteries."

The Mysteries consist of 3 groups pictured on pages 2, 3, and 4.

6. Meditate on 3rd Mystery, saying the "Our Father," ten "Hail Marys" and the "Glory Be."

7. Meditate on 4th Mystery, saying the "Our Father," ten "Hail Marys" and the "Glory Be."

5. Meditate on 2nd Mystery, saying the "Our Father," ten "Hail Marys" and the "Glory Be."

8. Meditate on 5th Mystery, saying the "Our Father," ten "Hail Marys" and the "Glory Be."

Meditate on 1st Mystery, saying the "Our Father," ten "Hail Marys" and the "Glory Be."

Say three "Hail Marys" and the "Glory Be."

Say the "Our Father."

Make the Sign of the Cross, say the Apostles' Creed.

9. Concluding prayers, "Hail Holy Queen" and "Let us Pray: O God, whose only begotten Son, etc."

The Family That Prays Together Stays Together

THE JOYFUL MYSTERIES

**1st Joyful Mystery
The Annunciation**

The Angel Gabriel appears to Mary, announcing She is to be the Mother of God.

MARCH 25

**5th Joyful Mystery
The Finding in the Temple**

The Blessed Mother finds Jesus in the Temple.

FEAST OF THE HOLY FAMILY

**2nd Joyful Myste[ry]
The Visitation**

Elizabeth greets M[ary] "Blessed art T[hou] among women [and] blessed is the fru[it] Thy womb!"

MAY 31

**4th Joyful Mystery
The Presentation**

The Blessed Mother presents the Child Jesus in the Temple.

FEBRUARY 2

**3rd Joyful Myste[ry]
The Nativity**

The Virgin Mary gi[ves] birth to the Rede[emer] of the World.

DECEMBER 25

THE SECOND STATION

Jesus accepts His cross.

SECOND STATION:

THE CROSS: SYMBOL OF LIFE

The symbol of the cross faces us constantly with the challenge of the cross. You said it plainly, O Jesus: "Take up your cross daily and follow me!"

That word 'daily' is what gets to us. If only there were some big work we could do which would satisfy both you and ourselves, even though it took ten or twenty years, and then to be secure. We all have that much heroism in us.

Getting up each morning to face the daily chores becomes so routine and boring. The trials and pressures of each day are like a grinding wheel. Yet, we must rise above these feelings and be happy with each day as a gift from God, to accept its special challenges and to spread the joy of Christian living to everyone we meet.

The cross is the symbol of an ALTAR, and we have our altars everywhere: a man's workbench, the kitchen-sink or stove, the desk at the office or school, a tractor or truck. These are all altars where we celebrate the liturgy with you. The liturgy of the cross, the liturgy of the altar and the liturgy of daily living are all one.

We are 'living hosts', each one of us. As 'living sacrifices' we learn to share our joys and sorrows and successes with each other, so as to become one liturgy with you, dear Jesus.

Teach us each day to take up that cross joyfully, to stand at the altar manfully and to celebrate the daily liturgy in a manner that is worthy of you.

THE THIRD STATION

Jesus falls the first time.

Third Station:

FIRST FALL:
THE TRIALS OF YOUTH

This first fall you suffer, Lord Jesus, can be compared with the first critical phase of our lives, the tempestuous time of youth.

This is the age of great insecurity, when we are held suspended between childhood and adulthood. We are so readily mistrusted, yet feel a desperate need for someone to trust. The flames of love surge up within us and we long for someone to really care, for someone to cherish us for ourselves.

We have a body which is keenly aware of its power to reach out to another's need, yet we experience the aloneness of rejection, by a parent or schoolmate who does not understand, or by a dear close friend who asks more than this growing, awkward body can give.

We have a mind growing into the wonders of knowledge and curiosity about people, yet meet some debasing dilemmas, from elders who hand us things instead of the help we need, or by an authority with a suspicious eye on everything we say or do.

We have a yearning heart, keenly sensitive to hurts and fears, to joy and activity and love, yet we feel constricted, by a society which considers us rebels or by a 'someone I care for' who keeps taking and asking for more, even to a betrayal of ourselves and God.

Lord Jesus, as you started your walk to Calvary, no one expected a fall, a failure, so soon. Right at the beginning, with all the potential ahead, you fall. How can you face what is ahead?

Can you go on? And can we go on with you! Can we together surmount the deep sense of insecurity, the feeling of inadequacy and the crushing despair of aloneness.

To continue the walk, we must first get up, as you did. Take us by the hand and let us walk with you through the moments of doubt and anguish which lie ahead.

THE FOURTH STATION

Jesus meets His mother.

Fourth Station:

THE ROLE OF MARY

Mary was always there when you needed her and at this crucial time she walks alongside you. She gave you birth in the flesh, and now, with you and your Spirit, she is becoming mother in a new sense, Mother of the Church.

It took a man and woman to start the human race and to cripple it by sin. It now takes a man and woman to repair the damage and to bring forth the new chosen race, the holy People of God, the royal priesthood.

Our baptism gives Mary a unique role in the lives of each one of us. As she was companion to you in life, especially in the Passion and Resurrection, so is she companion to each of us in ours. This is her special vocation: to be needed by us all. She is a constant reminder of our vocation as Christian: to be needed by others.

But why is it, Lord, that those whom you love must suffer so? Must suffering enter the life of every man who wants to be like you?

Must the wood be burned to charcoal before you can draw the portrait of a life?

The experience of Calvary and the reality of love make us realize how foolish are these questions. Love and sacrifice do necessarily go together. It is only in the crucible of pain and trial, of total self-giving, that love becomes selfless and fruitful.

It is because Mary loved you so much that she wanted to suffer and even die with you. It is because we love you that we want to share our whole life with your whole life, in joy and in fear, in success as well as failure, in good times and in bad.

Lord, teach us to be aware of the needs of others and to reach out for them in a spirit of love and sacrifice, not counting whatever cost to ourselves.

THE FIFTH STATION

Simon of Cyrene helps Jesus carry His cross.

Fifth Station:

THE CALL OF MAN

Now you invite *man* to take his place alongside you in the Passion and the Church and the world.

Simon of Cyrene was forced to help you. Most men have to be persuaded, even convinced by deeds. You had to prove yourself fully a man. Now I understand why you spent thirty years as a carpenter's son, to become one with us, to sanctify work, to consecrate everything we call ordinary. You showed us that there really isn't anything ordinary.

Man by nature is not ordinary either. Man is a dreamer. He thinks in terms of skyscrapers and bridges, of oceans and spaceships. He is drawn by adventure and urged by the sense of the heroic. He conquers by worlds.

All the great movements of history, both good and evil, were begun by him; the great spiritual and missionary movements, but also the great heresies and philosophies of evil. A man of virtue can be a great boon to the Church and society; a vicious man can cause great destruction.

And yet, Lord, why is it that so many men shy away from your message. They think religion is for women and children. Somehow we haven't reached them, and we must reach them if our Church is going to influence the world.

Dear Lord, our Church and world are bleeding right now. We need men, all the manpower we can get. Send us another Paul, an Augustine or a Benedict, a Francis or Ignatius. The world is fast eluding us by sheer numbers. You, the Christ, are suffering all over the world in the poor and the hungry and the enslaved. Raise up your saints and visionaries, Lord, men of great dreams and desires, who are men of action as well. With their inspiration your message will find its way into the hearts of men and your relief may be brought to the wounds of all.

THE SIXTH STATION

Veronica wipes the face of Jesus.

Sixth Station:

THE CALL OF WOMAN

The spontaneity of Veronica gives us an indication of the role of *woman* in the redeeming Church. She has a natural sense of faith and devotion, a deep intuitive grasp of the values of your message.

Woman is more of earth, more in touch with the here and now. She feels deeply with this sick child, with the neighbor who lost her husband, with a tragedy which takes place in the vicinity. Her emotions of love and tenderness and compassion are keenly sensitized. She moves first with the heart, then with the mind. She thinks in terms of hospitals and schools and playgrounds.

A mature and strong woman can do great things for the People of God. One who is selfish and possessive, an occasion of sin for others, can do great harm. Every great man has been cherished and inspired by sincere women. The downfall of every great man has been hastened by women who lost their sense of vocation.

Woman has always been the cradle of society now you and the Church are asking her to become evermore the heart of the world. She is the guardian of decency and modesty. Only when she wakes to the harm being done by evil-minded men will the morals of society be changed. Her basic tenderness will reach out to the poor and oppressed. Her intuition and sensitivity will prompt her to expose the evils of injustice everywhere.

Dear Lord, send us other Monicas, and Teresas, and Brigits and Clares. Give woman her true sense of dignity and vocation, a true sense of equality as an image of God. Make her realize the unique role she has among the People of God. Only when both men and women put their hearts and minds wholly to the task will the work of your redemption of the world be accomplished.

THE SEVENTH STATION

Jesus falls a second time.

Seventh Station:

SECOND FALL:
TRIALS OF MIDDLE-AGE

Dear Lord, this second fall is like a half-way mark to Calvary. We apply it to the second critical phase of our own lives, that of middle-age.

We tend to look back over the years and think seriously on what has happened. Some of our family and friends are missing. It has been a struggle to raise the children. Our work has often become routine and we desire more security. The risks of life and its many changes are fearsome. Many dreams have been shattered and we've made a lot of mistakes. But we do not want to go back and do it over again.

The great temptation during this age is complacency.

There is a complacency mingled with success. The person who says: I have a good job or business, everything is paid for, the kids are all educated, I have money set aside and plenty of insurance against old age.

But, Dear Lord, there is only one kind of insurance, isn't there? how we relate all these things to you. And you stated it plainly: "Seek first the kingdom of God and His justice, and all other things will be given you". And there is only one kind of success: how much closer we get to you in our daily living and how much we share of what we are and what we have with others.

Then there is a complacency mixed with frustration. The person who says: I guess I didn't do all I wanted to, the kids are grown up and gone, old age is just around the corner, I am beginning to feel the aches and pains.

Lord Jesus, make us realize that these are reminders of the reality of eternity. This is a wonderful time of our lives to deepen our sense of values and to find more time for the things of God.

THE EIGHTH STATION

Jesus meets some women from Jerusalem.

Eighth Station:

UNIQUE ROLE OF MOTHERS

These mothers sensed what an awful tragedy was taking place. Their intuition perceived the innocence and holiness of this Man of God. Someone would have to pay for this horrible deed and they were afraid.

It is a mother's unique role to give life and to respect life. These mothers with children cradled in their arms were protesting the evil of death and darkness, since they felt that the light of the world was going out.

In a deeply Christian sense every mother takes on every child in the world as her own. Being a life-giver herself, she cherishes all life, because it is from God. The creative instinct in her rebukes anything ugly and vicious, anything which harms young budding life of any kind.

The mother who turns on her own offspring to snuff out its life is a horror, a contradiction to everything good and beautiful you put into your own creation, dear Lord. Her selfishness shatters the family which must be the nest of holiness and virtue. It can actually destroy the society in which we live and move.

Dear Lord, you accepted their affection and sympathy, as a Man of God would. You also told them they sensed rightly: we must respond to a time of grace and visitation. The greed of their men-folk was leading to murder and darkness. So you ask them: "Pray for yourselves and for your children." A mother's prayer is a powerful force because it is so close to the heart of a creating God. They have often prayed a wayward husband into heaven or a prodigal child back to virtue. Their loving concern makes the children sense that the home is like a church pointing in the direction of heaven, where our real home and citizenship truly lie.

Dear Lord, make every mother see how her vocation is a priestly one: to give and nourish life, to pray for and stimulate God-life in her children and others, to be a creative force in the world.

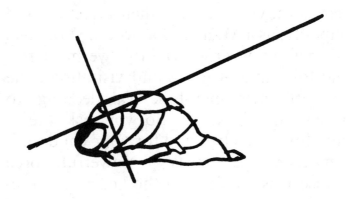

THE NINTH STATION

Jesus falls a third time.

Ninth Station:

TRIALS OF OLD AGE

Dear Lord, as we go into the later years of life another set of difficulties comes into play. It is the last stretch on the road home. Some worry about the nearness of death. Others look back on their shattered ideals and the mistakes of the past. Some are concerned about the evils of society and the excesses of youth. The most difficult cross of all is the emptiness and loneliness brought on by the loss of dear ones and the disappearance of friends.

The real Christians can adjust to these golden years. God has given them more time to pray and help others. Their wisdom and experience is a source of light and comfort to others. The sense of God and longing for Him become more acute. Each day reveals a new dimension and depth of God's grace and power. They keep discovering, they keep growing in the Spirit, they keep embracing more people in the ambit of their love. One day, full of maturity and graciousness, they give back to God the life He has given them. Dear Lord, give older people a sense of their special vocation. Let them realize the great good they can do by their example and inspiration and concern. There is no time to worry about past mistakes – they are forgiven. Now is the time to put the whole heart and effort into loving God and praying for others.

And dear Lord, may those of us who are still young not forget the aging parent or relative in the nursing home, the one we tend to neglect. And bless those who serve you in the aged – those doctors and nurses and associated personnel who look at wrinkled hands and sallow faces and minister to you in old age.

THE TENTH STATION

Jesus is stripped of His garments.

Tenth Station:

STRIPPED

Dear Lord, this is but the first in a series of strippings. They strip you of your clothing, the remnants of earth. Then you willingly let yourself be stripped of your friends, of a mother's loving care, and of a Father's consoling presence. Finally, you strip yourself of your own flesh and blood.

All of these you then give back to us: a Father, a mother, your own precious body and blood, and your special friends: the sick, the needy, the abandoned.

You had to be shamed in public to account for the shame of us all. Such a strange contrast takes place today: there is so little shame on the outside, but on the inside, the sons and daughters of men are ridden with shame and guilt. We have forgotten that you are our reconciliation and our purity of heart.

Teach us to be stripped of the frustrations and worries of life, and to help others with their burdens. Help us to think of those who are stripped of their human dignity: the old man in rags, the woman of the streets, the children orphaned by death or war, the dispossessed.

Lord, help us to value essentials, to strip from our world all that can be a hindrance in our work for you. When we look at a fellow human being, let us be able to see not black or red or yellow or white, not male or female, not young or old, but you incarnate again in our world.

When the time comes for us to be stripped of everyone and everything, may we be clothed in your Spirit and abandon ourselves fully to the will of our Heavenly Father.

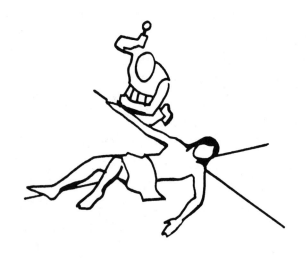

THE ELEVENTH STATION

Jesus is nailed to the cross.

Eleventh Station:

LOVE BUILDS AN ALTAR

Lord Jesus, you are the Divine Carpenter!
With lumber and nails and a hammer you
built yourself an altar. But why did you have
yourself nailed to it? Now it is you and the
cross alone!

You are trying to tell us something. You are
making it clear that no single temple is big
enough to contain you now. Our worship
is around a single altar, the cross. There is
only one victim, and that is why you were
nailed to it. There is only one high-priest,
and each of us in our own way share in that
priesthood.

There is only one baptism; one family of
God, the Church; one faith and devotion;
one liturgy with only one sacrifice; one food
to sustain us; one love which makes us all
one.

You laid your own flesh on that altar to
prove this – and it was consecrated by the
sprinkling of your own blood. You are the
total living sacrifice, the lamb who was slain

and is still alive. When you plunged that cross into the earth, you became our unity and peace and love.

True worship lies in the hearts of men now, in spirit and in truth. Our faith brings us more closely to each other than the members of a family. Sin is the great divider, the great disturber, because it is like a nail piercing your hands and feet, or like a lance driven right into your sacred heart.

Teach us, dear Lord, that our bodies are temples of the Holy Spirit. They are also altars on which we celebrate the daily liturgy with you. They are the 'living hosts' which we offer as 'victims' with you to our heavenly Father for the salvation of the whole world. As we share in your priesthood in this manner, let us become 'living sacrifices' in loving all men and in giving ourselves to whomever you bring into our lives.

THE TWELFTH STATION

Jesus dies on the cross.

Twelfth Station:

LOVE AND GIVING

"Greater love no man has than to lay down his life for his friends." You said it, Lord, and we made you prove it. Now no person can stand before that cross and be indifferent – we must commit ourselves with a "yes" or "no".

Even the menfolk who are convinced only by deeds take their stand. One thief cursed you and said "no" – he despaired, as Judas did. The other thief, who was your prisonmate, said "yes" – you finally won him over. The centurion commanding the execution said "yes". John, standing before the cross, said "yes". Even Peter from a distance said "yes" and "I'm sorry". The three Marys, standing at the cross and taking the place of womankind, had said "yes" long before. The crucifixion was the price of love and we know now that it means total risk and total giving. You said it for us: "If you lose your life for my sake, you will find it". A true Christian is one who has learned to love totally, to identify with you entirely, even to the cross, and to take on the whole world as his responsibility.

Dear Lord Jesus, your feet are nailed – take our feet to bear the message of your love across the part of the world where we live our daily lives.

Your hands are fastened – take our hands to give comfort and solace and service to those in need of you.

Your tongue is parched – let our lips speak for you the word of pardon, or of understanding, or of loving care.

Your head is thorn-crowned – take our human powers of reason and will and use them to express your word and your consecration.

Your heart is pierced – take our hearts to really love with: husband, wife, children. class-mates, fellow-workers, even strangers. our neighbors whoever they are.

Dear Jesus, help us to be witnesses to the truth that "love lives" everywhere in the Church and world of today.

THE THIRTEENTH STATION

Jesus is taken down from the cross.

Thirteenth Station:

THE PIETA

Dear Mother Mary, Woman of Sorrows, this is what it cost you to earn the privilege of being mother to us all. You walked to Calvary with Him; you drank the chalice; you did what we all must do, join ourselves completely to Him and His cause. Thank you for being so loyal to Him and to us. What a wonderful wisdom and love of God to have created you and to have given you this universal calling: to be needed by us all. What divine psychology for Him to know that we need a mother's gentle care all through life, so that we may ever retain the heart of a child before Him.

You are truly the chosen one, the blessed one among all women. You are the mother, model and inspiration of priests, religious and of all men and women, married or single. You show us what faith and love, and hope, and courage can do for the redemption of the world.

Why do some hold it against us because we

love you so? It was He, Himself who gave you to us as mother when He said, "Son, this is your mother".

Speak to Him about us, Mother Mary, and walk with each of us as we go through our Bethlehem and Nazareth and Cana and Calvary. Please stand beneath our cross and lead us to the New Jerusalem, to eternal life with Him and you and all the people of God. Inspire more young men and women to take up His cause as priests, brothers and sisters who can be a special sign of His service and love, as you yourself were. Help us all to appreciate our vocation, whether in family life or the consecrated life, and to give of ourselves and our lives to His work, no matter how hard it may become, even if love seems dead in our arms at times.

In the words of the Holy Bible and the Church, we make bold to say: "Hail Mary, full of grace, the Lord is with you; blessed are you among women and blessed is the fruit of your womb, Jesus. Holy Mary, Mother of God, pray for us sinners, now and at the hour of our death. Amen."

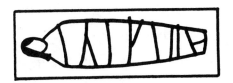

THE FOURTEENTH STATION

Jesus is laid in the tomb.

Fourteenth Station:

A CAVE AND A TOMB

The Light of the World seemed to have gone out for a while. The disciples are scattered, His friends are sick at heart and His enemies are terrified by the convulsions of nature.

They find a grave hewn out of rock, a tomb for a mangled body and a broken heart. All His followers thought this was the end of everything they had hoped for. Only Our Lady, Mother of the Infant Church, believed and remembered His three-time prophecy: "On the third day I will rise again."

O blessed tomb of Christ, which received His sacred body, do not try to contain Him, because you cannot. He has broken your seals for others – He will break them for Himself.

He has begun a new work of creation, and saw that it was good. It is the Sabbath and He is resting for a while.

For now, you are merely a repository.

Tomorrow you will be just another cave in the hillside. He is life itself, and you are the symbol of death. You are reduced to a mere threshold, the doorway to real life. The friends of Christ will walk through you boldly, knowing that on the other side the Divine Lover stands with open arms to embrace them for all eternity.

Dear Blessed Lord Jesus, there are moments of darkness and abandonment which reach us all at times, when faith seems dead, the idea of God seems dead, and the turmoil and change around us threaten to deaden our loyalty to you and our Church. Please send your Spirit to console us and enliven us. Give us the constancy of Mary to stand firm and to remember your words at the Last Supper: "I am going on ahead to prepare a place for you. Some day I will return and take you to myself, that where I am, you also may be. And your joy will be full, and no one will take it away from you."

EASTER

Jesus is raised to new life.

THE RISEN CHRIST

It is early Sunday morning. The power of God is here. The earth trembles. A flash of brilliant light! Life comes to life in a glorified body!

You break the seals of the tomb, Lord Jesus, and come forth in radiant splendor. The guards are terrified. Your angels are jubilant. You first appear to your loving mother. This moment is too sacred and too intimate, so it is hidden from us now, until such time as we merit this scene to be shown.

You appear to Mary Magdalen, the sinner, she who loved much. A touching scene in the garden where she calls you "Rabboni", "Dearest Lord".

Now it's Peter's turn. He sheds tears of joy and repentance, and you tell him all is forgiven.

You appear twice to the apostles in the upper room, that room which is haunted by memories. "Peace be with you!" you say, "not as the world gives, but as only I can give." The second time Thomas is there, Thomas, that rock-headed intellectual who has to see everything under a microscope. He succumbs and makes a beautiful profession of faith, "My Lord and my God!"

Here it is you show us the meaning of peace when you give your apostles and their successors the power to forgive sin. Sin it is that tears apart our world, our friendships and our inner selves. You are our reconciliation! You are order and harmony! You are our peace!

You walk down the road to Emmaus with two disciples who were probably going back home. Their hearts burn within them as you explain the Scriptures about yourself. They invite you to stay the night and they recognize you in the breaking of the bread.

You move in and out of your friends lives with all the delight of a young man just home from the battle-field of a far country. For each of them it is sheer joy to have you back alive.

Then that moving scene at the Sea of Galilee. Your men are out fishing – it seems, once a fisherman always a fisherman. You cook breakfast for them to show that even in your glorified state you come 'to serve'. That early morning you accost Peter directly and you hurt him, but it is a hurt prompted by love: "Peter, do you love me?... do you really, truly love me?" And Peter capitulates before Love itself: "Lord, you know all things... you know that I love you!" Peter has finally learned to love totally.

Then you take your whole family and all your friends to Mount Olive, another place haunted by memories. You give this final message and challenge: "All power is given to me in heaven and on earth. Go and teach all the people of the world and baptize them in the name of the Father and of the Son and of the Holy Spirit. I am with you always, even to the end of the world!"

RECOMMENDATION

This is one man's Way of the Cross. There are hundreds of other ways it can be done, since the Passion of Christ is inexhaustible. May these few thoughts prompt you to do it in your own way, and do it in many different ways.

Go through these scenes some time with the feelings of Our Lady. Another time see them through the eyes of John, or Peter, or Mary Magdalen. Try to experience them with the centurion, or the good thief, Dismas.

Finally, your own ingenuity can find other means to profit by this rich and age-old devotion.

May the Spirit of Jesus guide you in prayer.

THE SACRAMENT
OF RECONCILIATION

"Confession", "The Sacrament of Penance" and "Sacrament of Reconciliation" are all names used to signify the same reality. "Confession" was an early term used to describe this sacrament. It puts the emphasis on a proclamation of one's failures and successes in relating to God and to other men. "The Sacrament of Penance" is another term which, in this case, emphasizes the reparation and acts of expiation for one's sins. "Sacrament of Reconciliation" is the term used today. It emphasizes the positive notion of reuniting man with God and with others. At the same time, it speaks of God's merciful love in reuniting Himself to the repentant sinner.

In the Sacrament of Reconciliation, a person renews his commitment to live in the example set by Jesus Christ. He confesses his failings and his hopes for the future. He asks forgiveness of the priest who serves as the representative of Christ and of the Christian people. Through the power of Christ invested in the priest, the penitent is absolved of his sins, assured of God's forgiveness and forgiven by the community as well. The person who falls into sin harms himself and the Christian community, he also injures the love relationship between himself and God. The Sacrament of Reconciliation is the sign and instrument of reparation.

The penitent accepts some suitable penance to expiate the damage of his sin and resolves to lead a better life.

This sacrament must be received by any Catholic who commits serious sin. It is, however, of great spiritual benefit to all and the practice of devotional confession is both commendable and meritorious.

A sin is any thought, word or deed which harms the bond of love between God and man. It is a rejection of God's love inasmuch as God extends to every man the help needed to overcome temptation.

A serious sin, also called a "mortal" sin, is one which utterly destroys the bond of love. To be "mortal" a sin must be an action which the sinner himself believes to be serious; it must be fully reflected upon before the act and the sinner must fully will to perform this action knowing that it is a complete rejection of God.

Such a sin is probably rare and would entail more than a single action. A total change of attitude would be demanded in a man once bound to God and now seeking to reject God completely. Though such a sin would be rare, it is not impossible. If we fail to guard against temptation and lesser sins, we could be so weakened in resolve and in love that we would consciously turn to sin and reject God. This is why Satan works so subtly to persuade us into little failings, time and time again. This is why we must find our strength in the grace of God and renew it through His sacraments.

Another form of sin which we rarely think about is the sin of a community. Communal sins are often the result of a development over a long period of time, such as the scandal of disunity between Christian churches. At other times, they are perpetrated by the leaders of a people, as in the case of an unjust war. They might also rise out of the attitudes of a society as in the case of discrimination, prejudice and widespread immorality. More often than not, they simply rise out of a lack of concern for other human beings and for God's creation: the poor nations of the world cry out for justice, while the wealthy nations glut themselves, the unborn child is denied the very right to life, ecology is destroyed and resources are consumed without any thought of future generations of man.

It would be well at times to consider our participation in these communal sins, to do our part to offset them and to pray that they will end and that God will forgive us.

MAKING A GOOD CONFESSION

The more frequently we confess, the easier it is to make a complete confession and the more fully do we begin to appreciate the positive aspects of this sacrament.

As sinfulness is basically a question of one's fundamental attitudes, so also the Sacrament of Reconciliation should deal more in the expression of attitudes than in long "shopping lists" of sins.

It is true that serious sins must be confessed according to number and type. It is also true that fundamental attitudes may be indicated by listing our lesser sins. However, Catholic people have grown into a practice of repetitious listings of sins and have often left their confession at that. This is sufficient as a minimum but it would seem to indicate that little intensive thought has been given to changing one's attitudes and way of life for the better. It also makes it extremely difficult for the priest to give more than minimal guidance. He is there to serve the penitent as the representative of Christ and he can be more helpful if approached as a confidant and friend than as a grocery clerk.

Many new forms of the sacrament are now evolving and will help to instruct our communities in the positive and communal aspects of this sacrament. The essential form, however, is this: the penitent comes and asks for God's blessing. He then talks about his past, especially about the time since his last confession. He precisely indicates any serious sins he may have committed and also speaks about his progress and failures to live up to the example set by Christ. He may do this by indicating specific sins and by talking about his attitude toward God and toward other people. He then professes his resolution to do better in the future. The priest then advises him on ways in which he may improve his attitudes and gives him some direction for the future. In the process, the priest may ask some questions. He is not prying. Rather, he is trying to help. The priest then indicates some penance for the penitent to perform as an expiation for past failings. At times it would even be appropriate for the penitent to suggest his own penance, since he knows best what will be meaningful to him.

Finally, in the name of Christ and by His authority and power, the priest says the prayer of absolution, granting forgiveness to the repentant sinner.

The man who approached God in this sacrament is then fully reconciled to God and to the Church. He is renewed in grace and strengthened for the future. He is in full spiritual health and worthy again to bear the name "Christian."

Note: In the pages that follow, some points for meditation on daily life are offered as guides to examining our past life and to preparing ourselves for the Sacrament of Reconciliation and for the future.

POINTS OF REFLECTION
ON DAILY LIVING

(An Examination Of Conscience)

Divine law: "I am the Lord, your God, you shall not have strange gods before me."

Virtue: Faith

- Have I really accepted God in my heart as the very core and center of my being?
- Have I reserved my heart as God's sanctuary and not put up false gods in His place? Our "false gods" might be things like: money, sex, drugs, alcohol, tobacco, friendships, pet ideas and the like.
- Have I actively sought the help of God in times of doubt?
- Do I place my trust in God's providence for the necessities of life?

- Do I make good use of my God-given talents and abilities?
- Do I turn to God in prayer? And have my prayers been mere formulas or do I really communicate with God?

Prayer:
Father, you have made us for yourself alone, and our hearts are restless until they rest in you. Help us to seek first your kingdom and your righteousness so that all other things may then be ours as well. Forgive me for following my false gods. Give me light to know you and to do your will. Amen.

Divine law: "You shall not take the name of the Lord, your God, in vain."

Virtue: Respect
- Have I praised the Lord and returned praise to Him for His gift of creation and His goodness to me?
- Do I reverence the things and places that are dedicated to God?
- Do I show proper respect for the ministers of God?
- Do I show the same respect for the names

of God, Jesus and Mary which I show for the names of my dear friends?

- Do I live up to the name of Christ which I bear as a Christian?
- Do I place all my undertakings under the name of God?
- Do I call upon God to bless those who have been good to me?
- Do I call upon God to forgive and bless those who have harmed me?
- Do I strive to fulfill the vows and oaths which I've made in God's name?

Prayer:

Father, your name is another way of speaking of your whole goodness. How can I think of that name and not be filled with wonder and love? By the blessed name of Jesus we are saved. Forgive me for ever having taken your name in vain. Help me to respect your name, just as I want to love and honor your very presence. May your holy name be praised and blessed now and forever! Amen.

Divine law: "Remember to keep holy the Sabbath Day."

Virtue: Religion.

- Is the Mass, for me, a real communing with God or do I just "put in time?"
- Is the Mass a community celebration for me or do I shy away from full participation?
- Do I take time on Sunday to rest and reflect on God?
- Do I take time to read and understand the message of God in holy Scripture?
- Do I take time to prepare well for the reception of the sacraments?
- Do I accept the sacraments as the instruments of salvation, as the channels of God's mercy and love?
- Do I return to God a just portion of what He has given to me by helping to support the Church, Christian education and the poor?
- Do I thank God for His many blessings?
- Do I allow myself to become overly intrigued or entrapped by spiritualism or superstition?

Prayer:
Father, thank you for giving us Jesus, your

Son, as our Lord and Savior. Jesus, I thank you for the wonderful gift of yourself under the form of bread and wine. Forgive me for the many times I have failed to worship you, source of all love. I confess my neglect of you, at times my almost contemptuous disregard of you. Help me to renew my worship of you and my love for you in the Sacrifice of the Mass: for it is in the Mass that I truly come to love you in my brothers and sisters. Amen.

Divine law: "Honor your father and mother."

Virtue: Responsibility
- Have I respected legitimate authority in my family, on the job, in my government, and in my Church?
- Have I been negligent in the use of parental authority?
- Have I been helpful, without meddling, in the families of my relatives and friends?
- Have I been willing to make positive criticism of authorities with a view to helping them?

- Do I see all legitimate authority as a participation in the authority of God?
- Do I use my own authority responsibly, to help others grow, with patience, understanding and love?
- Do I trust those in my charge and delegate my authority?
- Do I handle authority responsibly and well, making it easy for those under me to follow my direction?
- Do I often complain about authority and seldom contribute to positive directions?

Prayer:

Father, you have said, "To obey is better than sacrifice." Pardon my disobedience. Teach me to grow in understanding, prudence and responsibility as I submit to the laws of my superiors, my Church and my country. Thank you, Father, for always watching over me. Bless my parents and grant them peace. Amen.

Divine law: "You shall not kill."

Virtue: Respect for life
- Do I respect the gift of life as a blessing of God?

- Do I respect my own life: physical, emotional, psychological and spiritual?
- Do I practice temperance and moderation in eating, drinking, smoking, exercising and the like?
- Do I make use of the ordinary means to preserve my health and my life? (Making use of extraordinary means is not required.)
- Do I drive safely as a means of protecting my own life and the lives of others?
- Do I have full respect for human life as yet unborn? And do I, thereby, hold the teachings of the Church in regard to abortion, and seek to encourage good prenatal care?
- Do I have a proper concern for the people who will inhabit this world in the future? In that concern, have I provided for my own offspring and have I done my part to protect and conserve the resources of this world?
- Do I make it a practice to visit the sick and especially the aged?
- Do I do my share in helping the poor and others in need?

- Do I control my anger and avoid inflicting unjust harm or injury on others?

Prayer:

Father, forgive me for the angry and resentful thoughts I often harbor against my neighbor. Help me to develop a proper respect for life and for the whole of creation. Help me to open myself to the peace of your Holy Spirit and to work for peace in the world. I know that my own actions which oppose the gift of life are unjust. Thank you, Jesus, for coming that we may have life, and have it more abundantly.

Divine law: "You shall not commit adultery"; "you shall not covet your neighbor's wife."

Virtue: Respect for human sexuality

- Do I see human sexuality as a beautiful gift of God and as a means of sharing in His power to transmit life in a loving way?
- Outside of marriage, do I channel the energy of my sexuality in proper expressions of love?

- Do I have a proper respect for my own sexuality and avoid abusing this special gift?
- Do I practice modesty in thought, dress, word and action?
- Do I avoid the places and things and people that exploit sex and tarnish its beauty?
- In marriage, do I avoid selfishness and mere self-gratification in the use of sex?
- Have I sought out pastoral guidance and do I have a clear understanding about the issues of birth-control and family-planning?
- Do I avoid the dangers of falling in love with someone I cannot marry?
- As a parent, have I lived up to my responsibility to educate my children in the beauty and dignity of sex?
- In guiding children in an understanding of human sexuality, have I avoided making sex seem something fearful or repugnant?

Prayer:
Father, forgive me for my sins of impurity and immodesty. It is difficult today to avoid

the temptations to impurity, yet you said that we would never be tempted beyond our means. You promised that we could grow stronger through conquering temptation. Thank you for giving me your help in time of need and help me to be ever more receptive in the future. Help me to maintain a proper attitude towards human sexuality. And, Mary, mother most pure, pray for me. Amen.

Divine law: "You shall not steal."

Virtue: Justice.

- Do I hold a proper respect for the rights and dignity of others?
- Do I respect the property of others?
- Do I avoid discriminating against others because of their race, religion, nationality, sex, age or personal feelings?
- Do I live up to my obligations in regard to my family, my employer, my government and my Church?
- Do I encourage others or participate myself in helping to banish injustices in my neighborhood, in my country and in the world?

- Have I made full restitution for any thefts or harm done to others?
- Have I made a will in order to insure the equitable distribution of my possessions after my death?
- Have I fulfilled all my contracts and paid my just bills?
- Have I avoided reckless gambling and unnecessary risks?
- Have I contributed to problems of pollution and conservation of natural resources?

Prayer:

Father, thank you for your creation and your abundant provision. Forgive me for so often using your gifts only to satisfy myself rather than to help others. I resolve to return anything that is not mine to its rightful owner, and to work for justice among all men. Let me live the words of your Son: "Seek first the kingdom of God and his justice." Amen.

Divine law: "You shall not bear false witness against your neighbor."

Virtue: Upright speech.

- Have I avoided participating in idle gossip?
- Have I avoided injuring the reputation and good name of others?
- Have I avoided invading the privacy of others and prying into their secrets and personal lives?
- Do I strive to be truthful in all my relationships with others?
- Do I offer fraternal correction to others. humbly and with love?
- Do I speak up for others when they are unjustly defamed?
- Do I make a real effort to defend the good name and reputation of others?
- Do I avoid falsification of documents, statements, testimony and recommendations?

Prayer:
Father, forgive me for the many times I have injured others by my uncharitable speech.

I'm sorry for the times I have lied. Help me to love others, especially my relatives and fellow-workers, by honestly discussing with them any differences we have. Heal us, Father, to remove our gossip and replace it with love. I ask this in Jesus' name. Amen.

Divine law: "You shall not covet your neighbor's goods."

Virtue: Contentment.

- Am I content with a moderate share of this world's goods?
- Do I avoid being envious of the possessions, talent or position of others?
- Do I avoid jealousy and possessiveness?
- Do I avoid wasting and abusing natural resources?
- Do I avoid the crimes of theft from embezzlement to shop-lifting?
- Have I been envious of the success of others?
- Have I been satisfied with my own success or am I greedy for unearned advancement?
- Do I trust in the providence of God?

Prayer:

Father, forgive me for having desired more of this world's goods than I need to do your will. Teach me to be content with what I have and to have a thankful spirit at all times. Help me not to covet the goods of others but rather to see where I can come to the aid of those who have less than I have. Thank you, Jesus, for giving me the example of your life. Help me to imitate you in your life of simplicity and poverty. Amen.

ACT OF CONTRITION

O My God, I humbly bow down before the heavens and the earth.

You are power, I am dust.

You are light, I am darkness.

You are merciful, I am sinful.

I am heartly sorry for all my sins by which I have despised You, forgotten You, displeased You.

Wash me more and more.

Jesus, mercy.

O My Jesus, eternal light, enlighten me. Eternal wisdom, teach me. Eternal holiness, sanctify me. Eternal mercy, pity me. Amen.

PRAYER AFTER THE SACRAMENT

O Lord, having been reconciled to you and to my brothers and sisters in Christ, I now ask that I may have the help to remain pleasing and acceptable to you. Whatever is lacking in me, now and at any other time, of sufficient contrition, or firm purpose of

amendment or personal integrity, may your loving mercy supply, and by it may you hold me more fully and more perfectly absolved: you who live and reign, God, forever. Amen.
(Paraphrased from *The Raccolta*)

PRAYERS FOR
SPECIAL INTENTIONS

GOD'S PLAN FOR ME

God has created me to do Him some definite service; he has committed some work to me which He has not committed to another. I have my mission—I may never know it in this life, but I shall be told it in the next.

I am a link in a chain, a bond of connection between persons. He has not created me for naught. I shall do good, I shall do His work. I shall be an angel of peace, a preacher of truth in my own place while not intending it—if I do but keep His Commandments.

Therefore, I will trust Him. Whatever, wherever I am. I can never be thrown away. If I am in sickness, my sickness may serve Him; in perplexity, my perplexity may serve Him; if I am in sorrow, my sorrow may serve Him. He does nothing in vain. He knows what He is about. He may take away my friends, He may throw me among strangers, He may make me feel desolate, make my spirits sink, hide my future from me—still He knows what He is about.

Cardinal Newman

FOR KNOWLEDGE OF AND
FIDELITY TO MY VOCATION

You have called all men to the Christian vocation, Lord, through the gift of new life in baptism. Realizing that this fundamental calling has many expressions, I ask for the eyes of faith that I may see more clearly the way in which you want me to live my Christian life.

Grant me the grace I need to live up to my particular vocation. Grant me the gifts of fidelity and perseverance. Help me to live with detachment from the material things of this life, that I may adhere more readily to you.

Help me to live with purity of soul and body, that I may give more fully of my love to you and to others. Help me to live in accord with the Father's will, that all I do may help to bring myself and others to everlasting joyful life with you.   Amen.

TO KNOW MY VOCATION

Lord Jesus, I know that you call all men to the Christian vocation in baptism and that this vocation is strengthened in confirmation. Still, the Christian vocation has many expressions and I pray for the enlightenment to know how you want me to live my Christian life.

Help me to see how I can best serve you; how I can put my God-given talents to work for others in your service. Help me to follow the desires which you provide in my heart, that I may know first of all whether

I am called to serve you in married life or single, whether in the ministry of religion or in the priesthood of the laity.

Help me to see how you want me to serve in that life, be it in the factory, office, school, hospital, church, home or whatever. Give me the grace and strength not only to know my vocation, but also to do my very best to serve others in my life and by so doing to serve you. I ask this, Lord, in your name. Amen.

TO FIND A SPOUSE

Lord Jesus, my prayer is quite simple: I want to marry. I want to have a really happy mariage. But, it seems I haven't yet met the right person.

Help me, Lord, to find the person with whom I can happily wed. Someone who will love me and understand me; someone whom I can love and understand; someone with whom to share the joys and sorrows of a full life; someone who is kind, thoughtful, patient and good.

Help me to find that 'someone' soon, Lord, if it is in the Father's plan. If not, grant me the grace of patience and the opportunity to continue to grow in my own ability to love, that when that 'someone' does come, I'll be prepared to give of myself and to accept the love of another.

Lord Jesus, I'm alone and I want to be two. Help me to forget myself for others that in giving myself I may teach myself to love. Then, Lord, grant me someone special. Amen.

PRAYER OF A PRIEST

Lord Jesus, you have called me to be your priest and minister.

Help me to give entirely of myself in your service.

Help me to give my body, even as it would like to give itself to others.

Help me to give my love to all without claiming anyone.

Help me to inspire affection and to direct it to you.

Help me to give of myself without holding back and without looking to receive.

Lord, I give you my hands that you might continue to bless.

I give you my lips that you might continue to speak.

I give you my body that you might continue to suffer.

I give you my heart that you might continue to understand and to love.

I give you myself, Lord; grant that I may be big enough to reach the world, strong enough to carry it and pure enough to embrace it without wanting to keep it.

Lord, stay with me; make me worthy to serve you.   Amen.

PRAYER OF A RELIGIOUS

Lord Jesus Christ, grant me the grace of perseverance in my vocation and to the vows that I have made. Help me to remain poor, chaste and obedient as you, that I may continue to serve you in humility and love.

Grant me the grace to remain faithful to the teachings of your Church, that I may be your witness to all the people you call me to serve. Give me the courage to rise above all pettiness and the honesty to know myself — that I may know you better and do your will.

Take me, Lord, and teach me patience in trials, resignation in weariness and joy in my work. Show me the wisdom of humility, the delight of union with you and the joy of being taken up in the labor of God.

Mary, Mother of the Church, pray for me. Amen.

PRAYER OF SPOUSES
FOR EACH OTHER

Lord Jesus, grant that I and my spouse may have a true and understanding love for each other. Grant that we may both be filled with faith and trust. Give us the grace to live with each other in peace and harmony. May we always bear with one another's weaknesses and grow from each other's strengths. Help us to forgive one another's failings and grant us patience, kindness, cheerfulness and the spirit of placing the well-being of one another ahead of self.

May the love that brought us together grow and mature with each passing year. Bring us both ever closer to you through our love for each other. Let our love grow to perfection. Amen.

A PARENT'S PRAYER

'OH, GOD, make me a better parent. Help me to understand my children, to listen patiently to what they have to say and to understand all their questions kindly. Keep me from interrupting them, talking back to them and contradicting them. Make me as courteous to them as I would have them be to me. Give me the courage to confess my sins against my children and ask them forgiveness, when I know that I have done wrong.

'May I not vainly hurt the feelings of my children. Forbid that I should laugh at their mistakes, or resort to shame and ridicule as punishment. Let me not tempt a child to lie and steal. So guide me hour by hour that I may demonstrate by all I say and do that honesty produces happiness.

'Reduce, I pray, the meanness in me. May I cease to nag; and when I am out of sorts, help me, O Lord, to hold my tongue. Blind me to the little errors of my children and help me to see the good things that they do. Give me a ready word for honest praise.

'Help me to treat my children as those of their own age, but let me not exact of them the judgments and conventions of adults. Allow me not to rob them of the opportunity to wait upon themselves, to think, to choose, and to make their own decisions.

'Forbid that I should ever punish them for my selfish satisfaction. May I grant them all their wishes that are reasonable and have the courage always to withhold a privilege which I know will do them harm.

'Make me so fair and just, so considerate and companionable to my children that they will have genuine esteem for me. Fit me to be loved and imitated by my children. Oh, God, do give me calm and poise and self-control.'

Garry C. Myers

PRAYER OF PARENTS
WITH GROWN CHILDREN

Lord Jesus, you've given us the grace of a long and happy married life. There have been many trials and difficulties — family differences, illnesses, financial problems and the like — but through them all you have helped us to grow closer to each other and to you.

Our children, signs of our love for each other and for them, will continue to bring us joy and a special pride. They will carry our life and our love to people and places we have not known. For them and for all the wonderful joys you brought into our life, we want to say 'thank you.'

Continue to bless us, Lord, in our life together. Stay close to us as we strive to come ever closer to you. You have lavished your love upon us and we wish to fill our lives by continually. offering our love and gratefulness to you. Thank you, Lord Jesus. Amen.

PRAYER OF A HOUSEWIFE

Mary, spouse of St. Joseph, help me in the task of keeping house, that it may always be a work of love and that I may provide a home for those I love where they will find comfort, understanding and love.

Teach me to find time in my daily work to think of God, to pray to him and to give him thanks. Help me to make work itself a prayer to God's glory. Help me to make my home and my heart another home for your Son, Jesus. Teach me to be as loving, kind, dignified and diligent as you were in your home at Nazareth. Mary, mother of Jesus, pray for me. Amen.

THE PRAYER OF A PERSON CALLED TO THE SINGLE LIFE

Lord Jesus, I'm leading a single life and don't plan to marry. Keep me conscious of the fact that leading a single life can be a special vocation. Help me to see with honesty and openness that my life can be one of great joy but that it may also involve great difficulty.

A single person must often face the problem of falling victim to self-centeredness, to great temptations against chastity and to the danger of never learning how to fully express love.

Grant me the help I need to be outgoing, to serve others, and to extend your love through my life to all I meet. Give me the grace to lead a chaste and holy life and the ability to express myself in my sexuality without going beyond the bounds of your moral teachings.

Be my companion. Guide me throughout my life. Strengthen me against all the difficulties which I may have to face precisely because I've chosen to accept the call to a single life. And Lord, bring me your love, joy and peace.   Amen.

PRAYER OF A WIDOW OR WIDOWER

Lord Jesus, moved with compassion for her sorrow and loneliness, you brought back to life the son of the widow of Naim. Now, with that same gentle compassion, please help me and all those who grieve the loss of a husband or wife.

Those who outlive a spouse whom they have long loved, see themselves disjoined from the only mind that has the same hopes, and fears and interests; from the only companion with whom they have shared so much joy and sorrow; and with whom they could set their spirit free, to retrace the past or anticipate the future.

Please help me to understand and to accept that the greatest love is to wholly desire the happiness of another, and that the greatest happiness is to be called to live in everlasting life with you.

Help me to realize that the love I experienced in my marriage need not diminish, but rather that it can continue to grow even through the sorrow of loss, and can continue to reach out and touch the lives of others who have never known such love.

Grant me the eyes of faith to see that I am not left alone, but am still together with my spouse — bound together in you, Lord, in your love and in your life.   Amen.

PRAYER OF A WORKER

Lord, Jesus Christ, I offer you today all my work, my hopes, my sorrows and joy. Grant me the grace to remain close to you today, to work with you and to do all that I do for your honor and glory. Help me to love you with all my heart and to serve you with all my strength.

Help me, Lord, to give a full day's work for a full day's pay. Help me to respect the property of others, to be honest in dealing with those involved in this task, and to put forth effort with personal interest. Give me the spirit of charity that I may contribute to the happiness of all those with whom I work and when the job is done, grant us all a peaceful rest.

St. Joseph, patron of workers, pray for me. Amen.

PRAYER OF A STUDENT

Lord Jesus, you are the Way, the Truth and the Life. Everything I learn in books, in school, in life is but a further grasp of you and all that has been made through you and for you.

My studies are difficult at times; so by your grace and along with my God-given talents, help me to understand, to learn and to continue to grow.

Give me, Lord Jesus, the gifts of intellectual honesty and clarity of thought. Help me to develop in my studies and to willingly share your knowledge with others. I ask this in your name, Lord Jesus.   Amen.

PRAYER OF A SICK PERSON

O God and Father, I offer you my sickness and suffering in union with the sufferings of your Son, Jesus Christ. You willed that he should suffer as he did for the salvation of the world. Let my sufferings, united with his, be meritorious for my salvation and that of others.

Give me the strength to accept my illness and if it is in your plan, may I be restored to health so as to serve you in holiness and wholeness. If not, give me the understanding to accept this cross, the humility to accept the help of others, and the grace to see your purpose in all the events of my life.   Amen.

FOR THE GRACE TO MAKE
A GOOD CONFESSION

O Lord, I want to make a really good confession. I want to be honest and open as the first expression of my renewed love for you. I want to tell you what I was and what I hope to be, that by my admission of sinfulness I will be cleansed and given the help I need to live in your love.

Sometimes I'm afraid, Lord, to confess my sins to the priest. Help me to realize that I can approach your sacrament with peace and joy; that I should fear only the evil of sin and not the confession which brings your saving help.

Help me in this sacrament of reconciliation to see not only what I have done wrong and what I have failed to do, but also to see the good things I have done, that I may do the same good things more consciously and more faithfully in the future.

Grant your priest the wisdom to show me your will, the patience to accept me with your own love and mercy and the understanding to help me with the problems and difficulties I have.

I am ready, Lord... to do your will! Amen.

FOR FORGIVENESS OF SIN

Lord Jesus, I am ashamed. I thought I was trying hard to be good and honest in dealing with others and with you, but now I realize that I closed myself to your grace; that I tried to go it alone, and now I've fallen again.

Once again I come to you asking, begging for forgiveness. I'm truly sorry for my sin, Lord... not only because of feelings of fear or guilt, but because I know that by sinning I offend the love that you have for me; I damage the image of God in myself; I fail to be all that I was created to be. I'm sorry, Lord. Forgive me again in your loving mercy. Help me to accept your grace to improve, to be good, to love.

I promise that from now on I'll look for the opportunities to do good; I'll develop a real attitude of self-giving love; I'll open my heart to your grace. I trust, Lord, in your saving mercy. Forgive me as I willingly forgive those who have offended me. I love you, Lord Jesus.   Amen.

FOR RESIGNATION
TO GOD'S WILL

Lord Jesus, in your agony you uttered the prayer, 'Not my will, but yours be done.' Help me to resign myself to the Father's will with such humility and love. Grant that I may perceive the things that I can change in my life; give me the help to accept those things I cannot change.

I know that you will permit only that which will lead to my salvation and that of others. Help me to accept the good things you send with a joyful and humble heart. Help me to accept, too, the cross which I must bear in union with you. I ask this, Lord, in your name. Amen.

FOR FIDELITY OF RELIGION

O Lord, I pray for the grace and the strength to remain faithful to your teachings and to the sacramental life of the Church. Help me to persevere in the commitments and promises I have made to you. Give me the fortitude to live up to the vocation I received in my baptism, to the duties derived from my confirmation in the Spirit, and to the graces received in the other sacraments.

Help me to place love of God and service to Him before all else and help me to bring selfless love to my brothers and sisters in Christ.   Amen.

FOR THE HEALTH OF FAMILY, FRIENDS AND SELF

They say, Lord, that 'Holiness is Wholeness'; so I pray for the wholeness and health of my family, my friends and myself. Grant us physical health, that we may serve you with full capacity. Grant us emotional health, that our service may be calm and loving and that we may never be ruled by our passions. Grant us psychological health, that we may serve with a clear mind and a pure heart. Grant us spiritual health, that we may pass safely through present sorrows and come to the joys of everlasting life. I ask this, Lord, in your name. Amen.

FOR THE GIFT
OF FRIENDSHIP

Jesus, I know that I'm never truly alone in this world; I know that God is always near and that there are always people around me. Still, Lord, sometimes I feel very lonely. Please send me a special friend, someone whom I can confide in and trust, someone who will trust me and be willing to share with me.

I'd like to have this gift of friendship, Jesus, so that I will be happier, but mostly so that I can make someone else happy too. Friendships are special, Lord, they make the people involved grow and grow closer to you. Send me a friend, Lord, and I'm sure I'll be a better friend to you. Send me a friend, Lord, so I can learn to love everyone more. Come to me in a friend, Lord, so I won't feel so alone anymore. Amen.

FOR THE GIFT OF PATIENCE

Sometimes, Jesus, things just get all bottled-up inside and I feel like I have to let off steam. Depression, frustration and anxiety seem to boil inside until I lose my temper, shout at the people I love, and say things I don't really mean.

Help me, Jesus, to be humble and patient; teach me to be more tolerant and gentle. And, Lord, when things get to be too much, grant me the wisdom to admit to myself that I'm on edge and help me to find a good and positive way to vent the energy inside myself.

Teach me in these times to look for that special act of love to do for others.

Mary, mother most patient, pray for me. Amen.

FOR THE GIFT OF UNDERSTANDING

Lord Jesus Christ, grant me the gift of understanding. Help me to understand the feelings of others, the desires of others, the goals of others. At the same time, help me to understand myself in my actions and reactions. Widen my vision beyond my own small world to embrace with knowledge and love the worlds of others.

Help me, Lord, to always see you at work in my own life and in the lives of others. Bless me with insight, acceptance and love that is tempered by you who are all things to all men. Help me to understand, Lord. Amen.

FOR PEACE IN THE FAMILY

Lord Jesus, my family needs your help today. We are searching for tranquility and peace and an end to discord. Give us strength and compassion to understand each other, wisdom and love to help each other and the trust and patience we need to live peacefully together.

Grant that through the intercession of your mother, Mary, and St. Joseph, our family too might become a holy family — a family that works together as one, a family that embraces peace and love, a family whose members are dedicated to each other and to God. Amen.

A PRAYER OF GRATITUDE

Thank you, Lord, for all your gifts of love,
especially for those we often overlook.

Thank you for friends — to increase our
love for you.

Thank you for enemies — to increase our
tolerance.

Thank you for joys and happiness — to
strengthen our faith in you.

Thank you for trials and tribulations — to
strengthen our trust and perseverance.

Thank you for the times when all goes well
— to teach us serenity.

Thank you for the days when things are
rough — to teach us patience.

Thank you for our successes — to increase
our confidence.

Thank you for our failures — to increase our humility.

Thank you, Lord, for the 'ups' and 'downs' of life.

Thank you, Lord, for the precious gift of life itself.

Help us to continue to grow and to learn, to love and to be grateful.

Comfort us when we are disturbed; disturb us when we become too comfortable.

Thank you, Lord, for being by our side.

Leo M. Kozeny
and
Father Mike Hanson, OMI

IN THANKSGIVING
FOR A FAVOR RECEIVED

Thank you, O God, for hearing my prayer and granting my request. Thank you for all the kindness you have shown me.

Thank you, Father, for your great love in giving me my life, for your great patience in preserving me despite my sinfulness, for your protection in the past and for the opportunity to serve and honor you in the future.

Thank you, Lord Jesus, for keeping me numberless times from sin and death by the toils of your life, the sufferings of your Passion, and by your victorious Resurrection.

Thank you, Holy Spirit of God, for bestowing so many graces upon my soul and for having so frequently renewed your life within me.

May my life, from now on, be a sign of my gratefulness.   Amen.

PRAYERS
OF RECONCILIATION

RECONCILIATION WITH GOD

SACRAMENTS

Lord Jesus, you have given us the sacraments as a supernatural means to help us attain salvation.

Through baptism we become children of God and members of the Church. Help us all to remain faithful to our baptismal promises and to grow each day in faith, hope and love.

Through confession, the sacrament of reconciliation, we are able to return to friendship with God and reaffirm our love for others. Help us to avoid sin and to trust in your saving grace and merciful love.

By the sacrament of confirmation we are signed with the chrism of salvation and given the strength to lead mature spiritual lives. Help all of us to accept the guidance of the Holy Spirit who leads us to unity in love.

In the eucharist, we receive the living Christ and at the same time give ourselves to Him. Help us to become more like Christ in our daily lives and, strengthened by the reception of communion, let us draw nearer to each other as we become one in Christ.

Through the sacrament of Christian marriage you consecrate human love and signify the unity of the Church. Help all married couples to remain united in love and to raise up families dedicated to you and to your Church.

By the anointing in the sacrament of the sick you restore the health of your Christian people. The renewal of spiritual health often leads to the renewal of physical well-being. Continue to strengthen us and to prepare us for the day when we must die to this life in order to live in the new life of heaven.

In the sacrament of holy orders you give men a share in the sacramental ministry of Jesus Christ, the high priest, and raise up servants and leaders for your priestly people. Grant that the ordained ministers of your pilgrim Church may remain faithful to their calling and may extend the work of Christ to all peoples.

Finally, you have given us the Church as an instrument and sign of our salvation. Keep this pilgrim Church under your protection

and lead it to final glory in your kingdom.
Amen.

CONVERSION

O Lord, from the beginning you have guided
mankind with your Word, Law and Promise.
Jesus Christ, the Word made flesh, is the
total expression of the Father. He has
revealed to us the Promise of our salvation
and the means of attaining it. All was created
through Him and from His cross He began
to draw all things to Himself in a new creation.

You gave your Law to the Jewish people
through Moses and fulfilled that Law in
Christ who extended to us the command to
love God above all and our neighbors as
ourselves.

You promised the people of the Old Testa-
ment that a messiah would come to establish
a new covenant in His blood. Jesus fulfilled
that Promise and gave us hope in the resurrection to come.

We have closed our ears to your Word. We

have broken your Law. We have lived as a people without your saving Promise.

Help us to have a change of heart, a true and lasting interior conversion. Bring us by the power of your Spirit back to the Word, the Law and the Promise. Bring us back to Christ that we may accept His gift of salvation from sin and death won for us on the cross. Lead all men, women and children to true happiness. Convert all of us by kindling within us the fire of your Spirit, the message of your Son and the fullness of life in God. We ask this in Jesus' name. Amen.

EXPIATION

O my God, so often have I come to you and promised to amend my life, to make up for the harm I have done to others and to sacrifice in expiation for my sins. And how often, Lord, have I forgotten that promise and returned to a sinful life.

I struggle constantly within myself to become the saintly person I want to be. It's as if there were within me the "ideal me" and the "bad me" while the *real* me strives for the first and clings to the second. Help me in my struggle, Lord, to be what you expect of me. Help me to change the things in my life that need improving and to strengthen the things in my life which are already good. Continue to be patient with me and to forgive me when I fall. I know that falling is not so bad as failing to get up and try again; so once more I promise to do better.

I promise to do my very best to avoid sin and to avoid the temptations that so often have led me into sin before. I will really try to make amends for the harm I have done to others and to approach them in love. Sometimes that's hardest of all, Lord, but I trust in your help.

I resolve again to make the sacrifices I can in atonement for offending you. I know I can never be worthy of your love and forgiveness, but by uniting my own sacrifices with the sacrificial life of Christ I hope to have some share in His promise of salvation.

And finally, Lord, I know myself; so help me when my resolution fades. In Jesus' name. Amen.

O Father, Son and Spirit, I pray in hope to reconcile myself to you, the Triune God. The bond of unity and love which is manifested in God is, for me, a sign of the love and unity in which I hope to live.

You, O Father, generate the Son and give existence to all creation. As the Son is your perfect expression, your only Word, help me to live in your created image and to express your goodness in my life. As you are the Father of all creation, help me to be creative in extending your loving concern to all around me.

You, Lord Jesus, are the Word of God and humbled yourself to become a man. You are like me in all things but sin. Help me to become more like you. Help me to banish sin from my life and bring me to a share in the divine life.

Holy Spirit of God, you are the force of unity and love between the Father and the Son. You extend that same unity and love to mankind in the Church. Help me to unite myself with others in the Church and to achieve true unity with God. Help me to learn from your love to love God above all things and to love myself and my brothers and sisters in Christ.

O Triune God, you have shown your unity to mankind, you have manifested your love in the whole of creation. Bring me and all men, women and children to a participation in your life. Let the world be renewed by the power of your love and let the new creation embrace all mankind.

To God be glory and praise forever. Amen.

RECONCILIATION WITH SELF

SELF-EVANGELIZATION

O Lord, I've heard a lot of sermons and I've even read your own word in the Scriptures. I've watched films and seen television programs dedicated to religious themes; I've listened to religious radio programs. Your message abounds yet somehow hasn't always touched me and certainly has never touched me as deeply as it could.

In one of your parables, you spoke about the seed falling on various types of soil. I pray that you'll make me a fertile garden, open and willing to accept your word. I pray that it will take root within me and eventually blossom in beautiful fruits.

I'm in need of "self-evangelization". I need to let your word take hold of me and renew my life. I need to really listen and not just hear, to really understand and not just see. You speak of love and I live without it. You speak of unity and I shy away from my brothers and sisters in the Lord. You speak of dying to self and my egoism barely withers. You speak of service and mission, of compassion and understanding. I tremble at doing more than the least and shield myself from touching or being touched by others.

Come, Lord Jesus. Take hold of me and bear me up. Guide me and lead me on, that I may live my life as a true Christian worthy of your name. Don't permit me to let my days run their course in humdrum apathy. Don't let my life be merely "time spent", rather let me live a full Christian life. Let me live the gospel! In your name, Jesus. Amen.

FOLLOWING CHRIST

Teach me, my Lord, to be kind and gentle in all the events of life: in disappointments, in thoughtlessness of others, in the insincerity of those I trusted, in the unfaithfulness of those on whom I relied.

Let me put myself aside, to think of the happiness of others, to hide my little pains and heartaches so that I may be the only one to suffer from them.

Teach me to profit by the suffering that comes across my path. Let me so use it that it may mellow me, not harden nor embitter me; that it may make me patient, not irritable; that it may make me broad in my forgiveness, not narrow, haughty and overbearing.

May no one be less good for having come within my influence; no one less pure, less true, less kind, less noble, for having been a fellow-traveler in our journey toward eternal life.

As I go my rounds from one distraction to another, let me whisper from time to time a word of love to you. May my life be lived in the supernatural, full of power for good and strong in its purpose of sanctity. Amen.

DRUGS

O Lord, the problem of drug abuse has become ever more serious in our day. It's affecting our children in their immature susceptibility to those who peddle dope. It's affecting adults in their immature dependency on drugs to help them cope with the problems of life. It's affecting our whole society through the unscrupulous people who push drugs either as a panacea for the problems of others or for their own profit. Drugs destroy the sensitivity of the users even when they are proclaimed to heighten awareness. Drugs can create a dependency, can destroy self-respect and can even cause death. Though no drug is evil in itself, it can become evil in the hands of man.

Teach us, Lord, teach all of us to avoid abusing drugs, to avoid abusing our own bodies and our own personalities. Guide us in the proper respect for our own well-being that we may have a proper respect for drugs and for their use.

Help those who are chained to drugs to find freedom. Help those who must use drugs to use them properly, sanely and safely. Help those who peddle drugs in evil pursuit of personal gain to realize the harm they do to innocent people and to repent of their sinful ways. Help pharmaceutical companies which produce drugs for legitimate uses to avoid excessive advertising and excessive desire for profit.

Lead all men into a fuller knowledge of the need to respect their own bodies, minds and souls. I ask this, Lord, in your name. Amen.

ALCOHOL

Lord Jesus, we often make fun of the man or woman who drinks to excess. We laugh at their actions and mock their intemperance. Help us to become sensitive to the deeply troubling needs of these people. Help us to sensitize ourselves to the problems faced by them and by their families.

I pray especially for the alcoholics, those who are suffering from a sickness and who are in need of treatment. Help them, Lord, to recognize their problem and help them to cope with it, so as to reconcile themselves within themselves.

Give them the courage to change the things they can change. Help them to overcome their desire to drink alcohol. Help them to overcome the problems they face within themselves and in relating to other people. Help them to restore their respect for themselves, their confidence in others and their trust in God.

Grant them the serenity to accept the things they cannot change. Grant them the strength to recognize their weakness. Grant them the fortitude to avoid being influenced by advertising and by the bottle in the hand of another. Grant them the patience to accept the problems they face in daily life. Support them when they are most in need of your support.

Finally, give them the gift of wisdom to know what can effectively be changed and what cannot, in order that they might adjust to life's daily struggle and come to full health. Amen.

HEALING

Lord Jesus, in your earthly life you performed many miracles of healing and yet suffered yourself for our salvation. This mystery of health and suffering seems a paradox. You indicated in your own words that the paradox is solved by faith.

Lord, grant us the faith to believe in the power of healing today. Help us to recognize your merciful power in the hands of the physician and in the words of the psychiatrist. Help us especially to see your healing miracle in the anointing given by a priest and in the sacrament of the sick. Help us to believe in the possibility of supernatural cures, be they physical, emotional, psychological or spiritual in nature. Help us to believe in your providence and in your desire for our well-being.

And Lord, grant us the faith to see how human suffering can be a participation in your own salvific suffering. Help us to realize that the crippled, the blind, the lame, the mentally deficient, all serve to bring salvation to the world by uniting their suffering with your own. Help us, too, to realize that our own suffering can serve as expiation for sin, and thus contribute to man's salvation. Finally Lord, reconcile us within ourselves by granting us the gift of health, and reconcile us to the Father's will in helping us to accept the gift of suffering. I pray in faith, Lord Jesus. Amen.

DEATH

I realize, Lord, that my own final reconciliation with you must come by the way of death. Help me, though, to reconcile myself with the inevitability of death itself. Help me to see beyond death to rebirth in God.

I know not how or when I will die, but be it fast or slow, difficult or easy, I pray that you will be close, and that I can find rest and reassurance in your presence.

I believe that those who die in Christ will be raised to new life. I believe that Jesus is the Resurrection and the Life. I believe that I shall live and never die the death of sin. as long as I remain faithful to you.

At the time of death, we celebrate the new life of the one who has died. Still, we also grieve the loss of a dear friend. Please support us who remain behind and comfort us with the knowledge that a person who died in Christ now lives in eternal joy.

You told us that those who mourn are blessed because they shall be comforted. We trust in your compassion and comfort; we joy in our newborn saint. We are confident that our greatest comfort will be to share one day in the happiness of heaven, reunited to our loved ones in our union with Christ. O Lord, I would also like to pray for all the living, that we might all be reconciled to our own need to die in order to rise, that we might be reconciled to the loss of dear friends and that, finally, we might be fully reconciled to you in heaven's joy. Amen.

RECONCILIATION IN THE CHURCH

RENEWAL

O Lord, with the advent of the Second Vatican Council, a spirit of renewal filled the Church. Changes in attitude and action have come about from the level of the hierarchy to the level of the layman. In this renewal many traditions have been restored and many new customs have begun. Theological studies have been reinvigorated and a search for unity, openness and love has been undertaken.

I realize that in any change, but especially in a dramatic and dynamic change, many people feel the hardship of a loss of security and, at the same time, lose the comfort of the "established ways" of doing things. I realize, too, that in a climate of change, some individuals get carried away in enthusiasm and "overdo it." Most importantly of all, I realize that Church renewal must really begin with individual interior renewal.

Please help all of us to renew our own commitments as Christians, that we might better serve our Church. Help us to adjust to external changes by changing internally. Give us confidence in our earthly leaders and abiding trust in the continuing action of the Holy Spirit.

Guide the Church to avoid excessive change in its search for renewal but, at the same time, let her be courageous in pursuing new approaches to fulfilling the mission of Christ.

Mary, Mother of the Church, you guided and protected Jesus as He grew from infancy to full adult life; guide us now, your children, as we grow into a fuller understanding of the Church and our own individual roles within the Church. Protect us from abuses and from harm, but lead us courageously into this new "Age of Vatican II." I pray in Jesus' name. Amen.

MARY

Almighty God, I accept Jesus as the unique mediator between God and man. In this role of mediation, He exercises His royal priesthood. The universal motherhood of Mary in no way diminishes His uniqueness as mediator. Mary does not impede the immediate union of faithful people to Christ. Rather, she enhances and fosters this union. Mary is our model of the virtuous life. She lived her faith in abiding hope and ardent love and, in this way, is a mother to us in the order of grace.

She accepted willingly to become the Mother of God and, in this way, she participated in a special way in man's salvation. She continues to serve in this salvific role as Mother of the Church, without diminishing from the dignity and efficacy of Christ, the one Mediator.

Help all of us who are members of the Church to contemplate Mary's sanctity, to imitate her charity and to fulfill the will of God, as she did, in our daily lives. Lead the Church to the perfection of Mary, that, by our lives, we may be an example of virtue to all.

Mary, you are a sign of sure hope and solace for God's pilgrim people. Encourage us to follow the path of your son, Jesus, that we may come to share the fullness of life in heaven. And, Mary, please continue to intercede for us, that all peoples of the human family, whether they be Christian or still unaware of their Savior, may be happily united in peace and harmony in the one family of God. Mary, Mother of God and Mother of the Church, pray for us. Amen.

HIERARCHY

O Lord, you have given us bishops as shepherds to guide your flock. As successors of the apostles, they continue the apostolic ministry of authority in the Church. They possess the fullest share in the priestly ministry of Jesus. They also have the power given them by Christ to raise up other priestly ministers in the service of the Church. United as a body with the pope presiding, and under the guidance of the Spirit, they manifest the will of God to the People of God.

The pope holds a special position as primate in the Church. He performs the ministry handed on by Christ through the apostle, Peter. This Petrine ministry is to guide the bishops when gathered in collegial unity and especially to signify the unity of the Church under one head. In this sense, the pope is truly the Vicar of Christ, for Christ is the Head of the Mystical Body.

Grant that our bishops may be faithful ministers of Christ and of His Church. Grant that they may always be open to the guidance of the Spirit, to the light of Christ and to the will of the Father.

Let the bishops truly signify the unity of the Church, especially when joined with the pope in collegial action. Grant them the wisdom to protect the valuable traditions of the Church and the dynamism to open new avenues to God.

O Mary, as Mother of the Church, I call upon you to intercede for the People of God that we may unite in spirit and prayer behind our consecrated leaders. Let us be patient with human errors in our knowledge that God directs the important affairs of the Church. Let us be vigilant in our prayerful support of the pope and the other bishops.

Let us be truly united with the hierarchy in a spirit of prayer, action and love. I ask this in the name of Christ who founded His Church upon the apostles. Amen.

PARISH

Lord Jesus, in our local churches, our parishes and missions, we strive to live as Christian communities. All too often, though, we don't even know the person who kneels next to us in your presence. As a community, we should be working in unity with our pastor to bring Christ to all the people of our parish. As a community, we should be joining together in public worship and praise of God.

Sadly, though, we seldom work together; we seldom even see each other except on Sunday; we seldom pray together. Rather, we each do "our own thing." Our efforts are feeble and scattered, our prayer is subdued and private even when we gather together. We even actually cringe when confronted with having to shake hands with the pastor or the man next to us in the pew. Most of the time, we are not a community at all. We are a crowd of empty faces carefully looking forward lest we meet the empty face of the person nearby.

"In the beginning was the Word." But, we are forced to ask ourselves if "in the Word there was a beginning." Help us, Lord, to begin. Help us to work together, to pray together, to be together in Christ. Help us renew our parish with dynamism and Love. Help us to follow the direction set by our priests and help our priests to give us direction.

The struggle in our parish to know and love each other grows from the fact that we hardly know or love the people in our neighborhood or town. We are divided by age, by race, by politics, by sex, by so many things. You are the Good Shepherd and you know your sheep. Bring your little flock together that we might truly know each other. Love grows in knowledge and the world will know that we are your disciples by the love we show for one another.

Renew us and help us to begin. Amen.

RECONCILIATION
OF SEPARATED BROTHERS

WORLD MISSION

O Lord, we can look upon our world today and still see many people whose lives have hardly been touched by the message of Christ. We can see those who have never met Him. We can see those who only pass Him by. We can see those who totally reject Him. We can see that the fields are ripe for harvest and that we have a mission from Christ Himself.

Help us with renewed zeal to do our part in fulfilling the mission of the Church. Help us to seek out, befriend and respect as brothers the abandoned poor with their many faces: the weak, the unemployed, the illiterate, victims of alcohol or drugs, the sick, the marginal masses in underdeveloped countries and the immigrants and minorities in our own country.

Let us never forget that the worst form of poverty is not to know Christ. Help us to preach the gospel by our lives to those who haven't heard it and especially to those who once lived it and now no longer see the need of Christ's presence in their lives.

Jesus, you labored throughout your earthly life to free men from everything that enslaved them: disease, egoism, spiritual blindness, death. By liberating within them all they possessed of value, you made them aware of their personal dignity. By dying and rising to new life, you gave all men the hope of a liberation that surpasses human efforts. Help us, Lord, to be free ourselves, so as to be able to free others. Help us to continue your mission "to bring good news to the poor, to proclaim liberty to captives." Amen.

CHRISTIANITY

O heavenly Father, your Son, Jesus, prayed that His Church might have a unity which was not merely spiritual but also material, a sign manifesting unity to the world. Promoting Christian unity is a duty of all believers, especially of those who are ministers of word and sacrament. Help each one of us to do our part in actively promoting unity. Help us to put aside bitter feelings and to concentrate on our common bonds. Grant the bishops, priests and ministers of religion the willingness to co-operate in the gospel mission and the courage to lead Christian people back into a single family of God.

The ministry of unifying God's people was a special part of Christ's earthly mission and He gave His unifying authority especially to Peter, the leader of the apostles. This authority and special ministry is accepted by Catholics as residing in the bishop of Rome. Grant that other Christian peoples may accept the necessity and validity of this ministry of unity. Grant that they may see the importance of acknowledging that Jesus wills to manifest this unity in an earthly minister, who by his very uniqueness symbolizes our unity under one head.

Bring us together in charity and in trust. Unite us in one faith. Make us one family. And, Mary, Mother of the Church, intercede for us that our prayers may have fuller value, as we pray for Christian unity in Him whose name we bear. Amen.

NON-CHRISTIANS

O Father, men of every age have looked to religion for answers to the profound mysteries of the human condition, which still today stir the heart of man: What is man? What is the meaning of life? From whence comes evil? What becomes of man after death? And, finally, who made this great plan?

Many religions, Christian and non-Christian, strive to answer these questions by proposing various "ways", which are composed of teachings, rules of life and sacred ceremony. In witness of our own Christian faith and life, we acknowledge, preserve and promote the spiritual and moral goods found among believers of other "ways", as well as the values of their societies and cultures.

Help us to be ever more open to seeing the presence and action of God in the lives of non-Christians. Help us to unite with them

in promoting virtue, prayer and brotherhood.

Guide our brothers and sisters of other
"ways" to the discovery of Jesus Christ, the
Way, the Truth and the Life. Help us to help
them discover the fullness of spiritual life in
the One Way. Grant them the strength and
wisdom to build on their own goodness and
values to the fuller life in Christ.

Grant that the Christian people of this world
may manifest true unity and joy in their daily
lives, in order that others will want to share
in this community of love and peace.

Lord Jesus, you told the woman of Samaria
that one day all men would share in common
worship of the Father. Grant that by our
prayers, our love, and our united effort, we
might soon achieve this goal. Bring us together
in common worship, that we might be fully
reconciled to God and to one another.
Amen.

NON-BELIEVERS

Lord Jesus, there are still many people in
our world today who do not believe. There

are those who, through no fault of their own, do not know of the gospel of Christ or of the Church, yet who strive to lead good lives as they search for God. There are also those who, without blame, have not come to an explicit knowledge of God, but who nevertheless strive to be good. And there are those, too, who have exchanged the truth of God for a lie, serving the creature rather than the Creator.

I pray for all of these people, that they may open their hearts to receiving God, and that they may have someone to bring the message of the gospel to them. Jesus, you came that all might be saved. Grant your Church the missionary spirit and the manpower she needs, to carry your word of salvation throughout the world.

I pray especially for those who have known God and who have rejected Him, and for those who have not known Him and yet have rejected their own notions of who and what He is. Grant that these poor people may be enlightened by the gospel message and inflamed with divine grace. Grant that they may repent of their errors and live in the Truth.

Guide all men to their heavenly home, that we may one day be reunited as one family with one God as Father to us all. May we live even now in the knowledge of God and in His peace and love. Amen.

ECUMENISM

In a world torn asunder by wars, hatreds, factions and divisions, the Church should stand as a sign and instrument of unity. Sadly, we are divided and our division is a scandal to the world. With this realization in mind, I join my prayer to that of Christ: THAT THEY ALL MAY BE ONE!

Father, may they be one in us, as you are
  in me and I am in you,
so that the world may believe it was you who
  sent me.
I have given them the glory you gave to me,
  that they may be one as we are one.
With me in them and you in me, may they
  be so completely one
that the world will realize that it was you
  who sent me

244

and that I have loved them as much as you
    loved me.
Father, I want those you have given me to
    be with me where I am,
so that they may always see the glory you
    have given me
because you loved me before the foundation
    of the world.
Father, Righteous One, the world has not
    known you, but I have known you,
and these have known that you have sent
    me.
I have made your name known to them and
    will continue to make it known,
so that the love with which you loved me
    may be in them,
and so that I may be in them.

(John 17:21-26)

RECONCILIATION
IN THE FAMILY OF MAN

FAMILY

Heavenly Father, you have given to parents the power of participating in your own creation. Through the creative love of parents you have given us the precious gift of family-life. I realize that the family is the basic unit in any society, and that it is through the family that the children of society are nurtured, protected and educated, as they grow in wisdom, age and grace before God and men.

Family life is often destroyed by internal strife, parental neglect, the fast pace of modern life and oppression from external forces. So I pray that you will strengthen the families in our society by filling parents and children with mutual love, by keeping the family bond strong and by offsetting the pressures which cause harm.

Let all our Christian families imitate the lives of the holy family of Nazareth. May all mothers have the patience, love and humility of Mary; all fathers, the gentle concern and fortitude of Joseph; and all children, the love, obedience and joy of Jesus.

Do not permit Christian parents to deny life or the necessities of life to their children. Rather, help them to realize your presence in their children and your providence in caring for everyone. Help them to educate their children in the values of Christian living and in the knowledge and love of God.

Let the family once again be the model for society and especially for the Church. Let it be the symbol of unity, the font of holiness and justice, and the nurturing environment for leading new life to maturity.

Grant, also, that one day we may all be reunited with the Father as one family, renewed and reconciled. I ask this in Jesus' name. Amen.

PEACE

Lord Jesus, you said to your apostles, "Peace I leave you; my peace I give you." I pray today for a participation in this gift of peace.

First of all, I pray for interior peace: for the tranquillity of heart to pass through the "growing pains" of personal problems to full maturity; for calmness of soul in the face of anxiety, frustration and temptation, and for stability in my daily life as I seek to live the gospel message.

I pray for peace in my family: the peace which only you can give, a peace that comes from a family life founded on faith, supported by trust and nurtured by mutual love. I pray for peace in the family of man, for more than merely the absence of war. I pray for a peace which truly holds the promise of progress, especially for those who are poor and suffering from privation of the very necessities of life. I pray for world peace in the hope that man can rise above petty differences and seek to develop international harmony for the benefit of all.

I pray that all men might come to share in the peace of knowing that you care and that you will continue to provide the things we need. I pray that all men might come to share in the peace of Christ which is both a present reality and a future promise.

Finally, I pray that all those who have died in Christ may now share in the peace of heaven and that all the living may aspire to participation in that same holy peace and life.

I pray in the name of Jesus Christ, the Prince of Peace. Amen.

JUSTICE

Lord Jesus, I pray for all my brothers and sisters, but especially for those who are on the margins of society: for the poor, the afflicted, the aged, the oppressed minorities. I pray for forgiveness for the crimes of injustice which are daily perpetrated upon these people. Especially do I pray for forgiveness for my participation in these injustices by my lack of concern.

The injustices I see among men, and find at times even in myself, are our failure to recognize and appreciate our brotherhood. Grant us reconciliation with our brothers and sisters in Christ, by building up within us a sense of justice, and an active love.

Grant peace and security, even now, to the poor and the oppressed, the underprivileged and the exceptional, those suffering from the ravages of war and from the natural disasters of earth.

Grant all of us the wisdom to deal honestly and uprightly with the minorities in our world. Help us to overcome the prejudices we harbor within our hearts. Let us not be guilty of stigmatizing anyone for any reason. I pray especially, Lord, for those who are suffering religious persecution and for those who, even today, are engaged in wars of religion. I pray for the people of Northern Ireland, for the people in the Middle East, for the people in communist lands and for the people right here at home who are looked down upon because of their dedication to God.

Lord, help me to support the rights of all men and women to live in freedom, peace and justice, and help me to do my part, cooperating with you, to serve you in my brothers and sisters. In Jesus' name. Amen.

CIVIL LEADERS

Lord, I pray for all government officials and especially for the leaders of my own country. I pray for the president, that he may conduct the affairs of national government with wisdom, bravery and true justice. I pray for the members of Congress that they may truly represent the needs of the people, and work in harmony for the advancement of all men, women and children. I pray for the judges that rule the courts of our land, that they may balance justice with mercy, and civil law with divine mandate.

Grant all of our national, state and local leaders the gifts of wisdom, justice, counsel and fortitude, that they may conduct the affairs of man in accord with the will of God. Grant to all men the gift of respect for lawful authority, justly exercised, that we may live as a united people, one nation under God. May all the governments of the world seek to reconcile power with the needs of society. May they all strive to form bonds of unity between countries, that we may one day share a united world of prosperity and peace.

Help each citizen to live up to civil obligations with a sense of pride, patriotism and conviction, that the governed may share in governing, and that government itself may be a bond of mutual support, trust and love. Let our civil authorities lead wisely and with concern, that we might all come, by way of peace and justice, to a new life under the divine authority, the source of all authority, God, our Father. Amen.

PRAYERS FOR OTHERS

FOR THE POPE

Lord, you granted to Peter and his successors the power to exercise your authority over the flock which is your Church. Grant to our Holy Father, Pope ...., the grace to follow your will in all things, the strength to resist the influence of worldly opinion, the wisdom to see your Spirit at work in men and in world events, the holiness to be an example for all of mankind, and the courage to protect your Church from evil in all its forms.

Help him as he works in union with the other bishops as shepherd, priest and teacher and grant him the joy of seeing the Church grow in numbers and in grace.   Amen.

FOR PRIESTS AND RELIGIOUS

Lord Jesus, you called the apostles to become 'fishers of men', now call ardent and generous young men and women to be your followers and your ministers. Let them share your desire to bring the good news of Salvation to all men.

Lord, I pray also for your priests and religious; help them to extend their horizons to the entire world where so many souls make silent supplication for the light of truth and the warmth of love.

Help them to remain steadfast in their commitment to your Church. Give them the gifts of wisdom and understanding and reward them with lasting peace and joy. Grant that they may labor without ceasing for the salvation of souls and above all for your glory. Amen.

FOR MARRIED COUPLES

Jesus, you saw so much value in the love between husband and wife that you elevated married life to a sacramental level. Marriage is a sign of the love and unity that exists between you and your Church.

Continue to give your help to married people that their love may grow day by day. Help them to realize that their love must overflow into the world around them. Give them strength in times of trial and difficulty; give them happiness, security and the joy of seeing their love expand beyond themselves to others. I ask this through the intercession of Mary and her beloved spouse, St. Joseph. Amen.

PRAYER FOR IN-LAWS

O Lord, I offer this prayer for my in-laws — especially for the parents of my spouse. Sometimes situations arise which can cause a lot of difficulty between us. I ask that you help them and me to be understanding and kind, patient and resourceful; so that we may always respect and love each other.

We are related by a marriage which symbolizes the love and unity between you and your Church. Let this marriage be the source of my love for them and the basis of their love for me. Let the bond of unity between my spouse and me be broad enough to embrace them, strong enough to support them when they are in need, and secure enough to stand firm if and when problems arise.

Finally, Lord, I ask you to bless them with your love, your joy and your peace.   Amen.

FOR FRIENDS AND RELATIVES

I want to pray, Lord, for my friends and relatives. It is through them that I come to know and love you better. I want them to be happy and to have all the love and good things they need. I'll do what I can to bring them these things, but I'd like you to show them special favor too.

Grant them health of soul and body; grant them peace, joy and happiness. Help them in the difficulties that they must face in this life. Keep them safe and keep them growing in love, in compassion and in understanding. Bring them ever closer to you. I ask this, Lord, in your name.   Amen.

FOR THE AGED

Remember your people, O Lord, especially those to whom you have given the gift of long life. Reward them even now for the good they have accomplished in the past; forgive them for their sins and failings. Make their last days happy and give them your grace, that they may continue to grow through the difficulties of their later years. Bring them and all your children through the sorrows of this present life to everlasting joyful life with you.   Amen.

FOR A CONVERSION

Faith, Lord, is clearly a gift of God. The beginnings of Faith can be found in Scriptures, persuasion, nature or people; yet, to know the Father belongs only to the Son and to those whom the Son chooses.

I pray, Lord, for the gift of Faith and the conversion of someone dear to me. You know us, Lord. Let us know you better, that we may love you better and that we may better conform our lives to your will.

He who sees the Son, sees the Father. Take away our blindness, Lord, that we may turn more readily to you. And help *me*, Lord, to be a better Christian, that I too might light the path for another. I pray in the name of Christ Jesus and through the intercession of Mary Immaculate. Amen.

FOR A DIVORCED PERSON

O Lord, you instituted the sacrament of marriage as a sign of the love and unity between yourself and your spouse, the Church. I know that you give married couples the grace they need to live together in love and harmony, yet so often the grace seems out of reach; love dissolves and the marriage falters.

I come to you in prayer to ask your grace and guidance, that a marriage may be mended; that the bond of love and unity may be restored and strengthened. Grant that the problems which led to this divorce may be the occasion for growth and that they be resolved.

If this is not the will of your Father, grant that all the people involved may see your purpose in what has happened and that they and all your Church may be forgiving and understanding. Lord, grant us all the gift of your Spirit, the Spirit of love and unity. Amen.

FOR OTHERS IN NEED

Jesus, I realize that there are people around me who are in far greater need of your help and loving kindness than myself. I want to pray for them, especially for those in greatest need. I want to join my prayer with theirs.

Keep me aware of the needs of others, Lord, and if there is anything I can do to help them, show me the way and grant me the means.

Listen to all of your brothers and sisters, Lord, and if it is in the Father's plan, grant their prayers without delay. I ask this in your name, Lord Jesus.   Amen.

FOR THOSE WHO HAVE DIED

O God, to whom it belongs to have mercy and to spare, I humbly pray for my brothers and sisters in Christ, for my relatives and friends and benefactors who have passed from this life. I beg your mercy, through the intercession of Blessed Mary, ever-virgin, and of all your Saints, that they may be admitted into everlasting life with you and may have a share in your eternal happiness. I ask this in Jesus' name. Amen.

FOR PEACE OF MIND

Lord, Jesus Christ, I'm upset and disturbed and I pray that you will grant me the grace of inner peace. As you commanded the storm winds at sea to be calm, command the storms of my passions and, by your grace, calm my proneness to love created things too much. Give me a love of suffering for your sake. Make me tolerant and kind to others, that I may avoid quarrels and arguments. Teach me to seek after and acquire that perfect resignation to the Father's will which alone brings peace of mind and peace of heart. Amen.

FOR SUFFICIENT AND STEADY WORK

Lord Jesus, I'm in need of a steady job with sufficient wage earnings to care for and support myself and others. I want to work to make a decent living, yet it's so hard to find a respectable job.

You have said, 'Ask and it will be given to you; seek and you shall find; knock and it will be opened to you'. Please, Lord, I ask you for the opportunity to serve you in some area of life that will help in my support and that of others.

I'm not asking for a job that flatters my pride. I'm willing to do your will in humble ways. I promise I'll work conscientiously and share your blessings with others, if you will only answer my prayer. I place my trust in you, resigned to your will. Amen.

FOR A SPECIAL GRACE

Jesus, I come to you seeking a special grace, a special favor, to help me to live a more Christian life. I can't achieve what I desire through my own efforts, yet with your help I can accomplish all.

Pour your grace upon me not only to cleanse and elevate this life of mine but also, if it be in the Father's plan, to make my life happier, humbler, more Christ-like.

Grant that I may learn to love you more, to serve you more faithfully, and to give more willingly of myself in service of others. Hear my prayer, O Lord, and grant me your grace.   Amen.

FOR A SPECIAL INTENTION

I pray to you, O Lord, for a very special intention: .... You promised us that whatever we asked for in your name would be granted. I know I cannot force your hand but if my request is not opposed to your Father's will, please hear and answer me. I, for my part, will do what I can, Lord, but without your help I can accomplish nothing.

Grant that my will may always be one with the Father's and grant me the resignation of spirit to accept with joy whatever he decrees. I ask this in your name, Lord Jesus. Amen.

PRAYER FOR A PERSON ONE DISLIKES

Although some people seem on the surface to be quite awful through and through, Lord, I know that this can't be so. There must be something tremendously worthwhile in the worst of us or you would never have bothered to create and redeem us. Let me, then, see others as *you* see them, let me look for those sides in their characters which are attractive and, even—unlikely as it may seem—beautiful. I have someone in mind, Lord, whom I want to see in a good light instead of in a bad one as at present. I pray for that soul as I would pray for a person I really felt I loved. I want to be able to benefit that soul; I must look for occasions of going against my personal dislike and actually showing charity to that soul. For *your* sake, I want to love where, if left to myself, I would heartily detest. Lord, who are love itself, help me in this.   Amen.

Don Hubert van Zeller, OSB

270

FOR A SOLUTION TO AN
ALCOHOLIC PROBLEM

Lord Jesus, you know the problems that are suffered by the alcoholic and by those who must live with an alcoholic. You know how I am suffering with this problem now.

In your life in Galilee and Jerusalem you undoubtedly met and dealt with people who had this problem. I pray for the grace and the strength to learn how to deal with the problem in my life. I seek not only the gift of toleration and patience but a real and lasting solution.

So many lives are hurt and even ruined by the problem of alcoholism. I want you to spare these lives by granting your help. Grant the gift of lasting health, that all of us might serve you better. I ask this, Lord, in your name.   Amen.

FOR A SOLUTION TO
A DRUG PROBLEM

The gift of drugs was given to us by you, Father, and in your plan of creation they are good. Yet, some of us have been weak and intemperate in their use and have become their slave.

When I see the de-humanizing effects of drugs ill-used, I can but turn to you and beg for a lasting solution to the drug problem as it touches my life.

Help me to learn where to go for help and what must be done and give me the strength to do it. Grant also that the illegal supplies and the pushers be stopped. Protect us from the evils created by the bad usage of drugs. And grant your help and protection to all who have fallen under their influence. I ask this in your name and in the name of your Son, Christ our Lord. Amen.

FOR SOCIAL JUSTICE

O Father, I want to pray for all of my brothers and sisters in Christ. The injustices I see among men, and at times find even in myself, are our failure to appreciate and recognize our brotherhood.

Grant peace and security, even now, to the poor and the persecuted, the underprivileged, the exceptional, those suffering from the ravages of war and the natural disasters of earth. Grant us the wisdom to deal honestly and uprightly with the minorities in our world. Help us to overcome the prejudices we harbor within ourselves. Let us not be guilty of stigmatizing anyone for any reason.

Help me to realize the equality of all men and women in their rights of life, freedom and happiness in this world and in the next. May I do my part, cooperating with you, to serve you in my brothers and sisters. Amen.

FOR TRAVELERS

Lord God, you watch over all our ways. Guide us and guard us especially while we travel. Keep us mindful of the precious gift of life which we have received from you, that we may not come to harm nor be guilty of harming others.

Help us to remain alert and careful along the way. Help the one who drives to be mindful of the rules of safety and of common sense. Bring us safely to this journey's end and let this prayer be our inspiration both upon the road and throughout our lives.

Mary, our mother, watch over us on our way, for all your ways are calm and all your paths are peace. Stay with us now and always. Amen.

FOR AN UNWED MOTHER
AND HER CHILD

I pray, O Lord, with compassion for a mother and her child. The mother needs great courage and great love; the child needs not only a mother's care but acceptance and a family's love.

Grant them both, O Lord, the grace they need to grow, the strength they need to live, and the understanding and kindness of others to bring peace to their troubled lives.

Stay close to them, Lord, and see that the need of a husband's and father's love is somehow provided. Bring them your grace, your love, your peace and joy.

May they be taken under the protection of your mother, Mary, and St. Joseph, that they might share in all the goodness and kindness of your holy family.   Amen.

FOR A DELINQUENT CHILD

Lord Jesus, you asked your apostles to let
the little children come to you and you laid
your hands on them and blessed them. I
ask you now to take a child into your care
and to grant this child your grace and
blessings.

Time and circumstances have contributed to
forming this child, and some of that for-
mation has not been good. People, too, have
influenced this child and I ask now that
only the good influences may prevail.

Help me to help this child. Help me to find the proper things to do to change his (her) life for the better. Help me to be a trustworthy friend and a good example for this child, that he (she) may grow in wisdom and grace.

Grant that those people, places and events that have led him (her) away from a good Christian life may no longer have any influence or sway. Let this, my child, come to you.   Amen.

FOR THE CRIPPLED AND
CHRONICALLY ILL

Lord Jesus, you have chosen some of us to share in a special way in your sufferings for the salvation of the world. Help those who share your sufferings in the body by giving them renewed life in their souls.

Let them realize the value and power that comes from their suffering, from their vocation to contribute to the salvation of all men. Help them to be strong and courageous as they share in your work of atonement. Let them be a sign for all of us of the strength of your grace. And grant them happiness and joy in their knowledge of serving you.

And, Lord, if it be in the Father's plan, grant health in body to those too weak to bear this cross, and also to those so strong in faith that their cure would witness to your glory and love. Amen.

FOR A SOLUTION TO A
FINANCIAL PROBLEM

Lord Jesus, when you instructed your apostle, Peter, to take the tax-money from the mouth of a fish, you taught us to rely on the providence of God to supply our earthly needs. You taught us the same lesson from the lilies of the field and the birds of the air.

Lord, I must rely now on your promise to help, because I'm in financial trouble. I've done what I can do to acquire honestly what I need, but the problem remains. Help me to find the right road to earthly security, as I promise to rely on you always for my spiritual security.

Grant me what I need in this life, that I may care for myself and share your blessings with others. Help me in all my needs, material and spiritual. I place my confident trust in you, O Lord.   Amen.

FOR CHURCH UNITY

Heavenly Father, we have all sinned. In some way we are responsible for Christian disunity. Teach us to embrace together the life and teachings of your Son.

Lord Jesus, make me more Christ-like, so that by my prayers and good works I may be a help to full unity among all who call on the Name of Jesus.

Spirit of Love and Unity, give us a change of heart, that we might bridge the gaps that separate us and surmount the barriers that divide us.

Mary, Mother of the Church, pray for us — pray for the unity of all Christian people. Amen.

FOR CHILDREN

Jesus, you asked for the little children to be brought to you; so I bring my children to you in prayer. I ask you to bless them, to make them strong and healthy. Fill them with your grace and with your love. Stay with them as they grow to maturity and help them to learn the virtues of kindness, humility, peace, patience, love, wisdom and understanding.

Let their parents and teachers be good examples for them; let their friendships be good and valuable; let their knowledge of and love for you continue to grow day by day. Grant them a happy life — now, and in eternity.   Amen.

PRAYER FOR PRIESTS

Almighty God, Father, Son and Holy
   Spirit!
  Increase the number of our priests!
Make them strong in faith,
  always alert to your people's needs,
  ever profoundly spiritual,
    understanding and charitable.
Grant to priests zeal in their vocation,
  success in their labors.
May they do all things for love of You and
  love of neighbor. Amen.
Pray for priests, O Holy Mother of God,
  that they may be made worthy
    of the promises of Christ. Amen.

Anonymous

PRAYER OF ST. FRANCIS

Lord, make me an instrument of your
     peace,
Where there is hatred, let me sow love,
Where there is injury, pardon;
Where there is discord, union;
Where there is doubt, faith;
Where there is despair, hope;
Where there is darkness, light;
And where there is sadness, joy.

O Master, grant that I may not so much
     seek to be consoled as to console;
To be understood, as to understand;
To be loved, as to love;
For it is in giving that we receive.
It is in pardoning that we are pardoned;
And it is in dying that we are born to
     eternal life.

(St. Francis of Assisi)

FOR PEACE IN THE WORLD

Lord Jesus Christ, Prince of Peace, grant us peace throughout the world, that all nations may work together and that there might be an end to war. I ask this, Lord, in your name.   Amen.

PICTURE IDENTIFICATION - [All pictures are at the National Shrine of Our Lady of the Snows, Belleville, Ill.] - at right, participants at weekly Candlelight Procession; inside back cover: left page, the Agony Garden; right page, Way of the Cross.